Cooperative Learning and Strategies for Inclusion

Celebrating Diversity in the Classroom

edited by

JoAnne W. Putnam, Ph.D.
Associate Professor
and Interim Chair
School of Education
University of Alaska, Anchorage

·P A U L·H·
BROOKES
PUBLISHING Co

Baltimore • London • Toronto • Sydney

Paul H. Brookes Publishing Co.
P.O. Box 10624
Baltimore, MD 21285-0624

Typeset by Brushwood Graphics, Inc., Baltimore, Maryland.
Manufactured in the United States of America by
BookCrafters, Falls Church, Virginia.

While the situations and experiences described in this book are real, the names of
individual students have been changed.

This book is printed on recycled paper. ♲

Library of Congress Cataloging-in-Publication Data

Cooperative learning and strategies for inclusion : celebrating diversity in the
classroom / edited by JoAnne W. Putnam.
    p.   cm.—(Children, youth & change)
Includes bibliographical references and index.
ISBN 1-55766-134-0
1. Mainstreaming in education—United States.   2. Special education—
United States.   3. Handicapped children—Education—United States.
4. Intercultural education—United States.   I. Putnam, JoAnne W.
(JoAnne Wachholz)   II. Series.
LC4019.C58   1993   93-428
371.9'046'0973—dc20   CIP

British Library Cataloguing-in-Publication data are available from the British
Library.

Series Editors:
Luanna H. Meyer, Ph.D.
Cheryl A. Utley, Ph.D.

Cooperative Learning
an Strategies
Inclusion

ii

Contents

Contributors

THE EDITOR

JoAnne W. Putnam, Ph.D., Associate Professor and Interim Chair of Special Education, University of Alaska, Anchorage, 3211 Providence Drive, Anchorage, Alaska 99508

JoAnne Putnam was a special education teacher before earning her doctorate at the University of Minnesota in 1983. She is currently Associate Professor of Special Education at the University of Alaska, Anchorage. Her research and writings focus on cooperative learning, teaching in inclusive classrooms, and de-institutionalization. She is actively involved in promoting school–university partnerships for educational reform, distance education, and consulting with teachers nationally and abroad about cooperative learning, instructional strategies, autism, and inclusion.

THE CHAPTER AUTHORS

Leah A. Henry, M.S., Research Assistant and Doctoral Candidate, Special Education Programs, Syracuse University, Syracuse, New York 13244-2280

Leah Henry's research interests include social relationships among children and youth with and without disabilities, students considered to be at risk of leaving school prior to high school graduation, and inclusive schooling.

Jo Jakupcak, M.Ed., Doctoral Candidate, University of Montana, Missoula, Montana 59801

Jo Jakupcak's work has focused on whole language instructional techniques, inclusive education, and curriculum improvement for all students through the development of metacognitive skills within the regular classroom.

Luanna H. Meyer, Ph.D., Professor of Education, Syracuse University, Syracuse, New York 13244-2280

Luanna Meyer is coordinator of the Inclusive Elementary and Special Education Teacher Preparation Program and the director of the Consortium for Collaborative Research on Social Relationships of Children and Youth. Her research and publications have focused on children's social relationships, positive approaches to challenging behaviors, and theoretical and practical issues surrounding the implementation of innovative practices in education.

Ann Nevin, Ph.D., Professor of Education, Arizona State University West, P.O. Box 37100, Phoenix, Arizona 85069-7100

Ann Nevin is a professor and coordinator of the teacher education programs at Arizona State University West. Her research focuses on discovering and validating what teachers can do to effectively accelerate the academic and social progress of learners with disabilities. She is an internationally recognized expert in collaborative consultation and the integration of learners with disabilities into the general education classroom. She helped establish the Vermont Consulting Teacher Program, an innovative system to help classroom teachers and special educators plan, implement, and evaluate instruction for students with disabilities in general education classes. As a national leadership trainer in cooperative learning, she has experimentally as well as experientially validated cooperative learning approaches to the inclusion of students with disabilities.

Loraine J. Spenciner, Ph.D., Associate Professor of Early Childhood Special Education, University of Maine at Farmington, Farmington, Maine 04009

Loraine Spenciner facilitates the Early Intervention Play Group for Children and Families, a collaborative project between the University of Maine at Farmington and Maine's Bureau of Children with Special Needs. Her current research focuses on assessment issues and the use of assistive technology.

Jacqueline S. Thousand, Ph.D., Research Associate Professor, Center for Developmental Disabilities, College of Education, 449 C Waterman Building, University of Vermont, Burlington, Vermont 05401

Since 1986, Jacqueline Thousand has coordinated a graduate training program that prepares *Integration Facilitators,* advanced educational leadership personnel who work with administrators, teachers, and families to redesign the delivery of special education services so that learners with extensive educational and psychological challenges experience quality educational and social opportunities within their local general education and community environments. Dr. Thousand's most recent research is in the areas of collaborative consultation and teaming, school-based systems change strategies, cooperative group learning and partner learning, transition planning, attitudinal change strategies, and international educational exchange.

Richard A. Villa, Ph.D., President, Bayridge Educational Consortium, 6 Bayridge Estates, Colchester, Vermont 05446

Richard Villa's primary field of expertise is the development of administrative support systems for educating all students within general education settings. Dr. Villa has taught a number of subjects at both the middle and secondary school levels, including biology, chemistry, physics, government, and special education; his administrative experiences include serving as a special education administrator, pupil personnel services director, and director of instructional services. Dr. Villa is currently president of the Bayridge Educational Consortium and an adjunct professor at the University of Vermont and St. Michael's College; he teaches courses and supervises practica in the development of effective administrative and instructional skills for accommodating all students within general education classrooms.

Dilafruz R. Williams, Ph.D. Assistant Professor of Educational Policy, Foundations, and Administrative Studies, Portland State University, P.O. Box 751, Portland, Oregon 97207-0751

Dilafruz Williams is interested in the moral issues related to inclusion. Her research is in the area of the nature and formation of communities in urban schools, primarily at the middle school level. She is the president of Wholistic Education, a special interest group of the American Education Research Association.

Preface

*C*ooperative Learning and Strategies for *Inclusion: Celebrating Diversity in the Classroom* is the first volume in the new *Children, Youth & Change: Sociocultural Perspectives* book series. This series will address the critical new imperatives challenging the social systems of today's world. The impetus for these volumes is the fact that our existing literature does not accurately reflect the exciting diversity of our changing population. Because so many factors affect children's growth and development, contributions to the series will come from a variety of fields, including medicine, anthropology, sociology, economics, public health, psychology, child development, special education, teacher education, and other academic disciplines. Thus, the series will be multidisciplinary and open to a wide range of perspectives and approaches that foster understanding of how best to meet the needs of children and youth in today's changing world.

Demographic trends suggest that by the year 2000, one third of our nation will be members of ethnic and minority groups, by 2020, 39% of the school-age population will be minority, and by 2060, this figure will reach 60% (American Council on Education, 1988). This inaugural volume in the series highlights the growing use of cooperative learning—one powerful method for enabling children to celebrate and benefit from the diversity that characterizes our schools, communities, and society. Cooperative learning is an approach compatible with diverse cultural groups and one that exposes all students to a variety of methods for learning. It encourages children to respect and value one another (Nieto, 1992). In a cooperative learning environment, every student has the opportunity to learn more effectively.

Although the series is not restricted to educational topics, it appears most fitting that the first contribution to *Children, Youth & Change: Sociocultural Perspectives* is focused on one of the most promising instructional strategies for enhancing children's sociopersonal growth and development in school, which is one of the primary social systems in most children's lives, with the power to either improve or harm their sense of self and their interpersonal relationships. Effective schools must recognize the full context of schooling (i.e., social, cultural, and political environment) and the ways that the elements of this context affect student achievement and social development across the lifespan. The central role of school personnel is to provide a supportive environment, one that takes into account the influence of educational resources, student qualities, instructional elements, and other factors in the school's context and process (Cortés, 1981). Today's schools must teach more than academic skills: outside of the family, school is the primary setting children learn about their own place in the world.

Cooperative Learning and Strategies for Inclusion is designed to assist educators in meeting the needs of a diversity of learners—children with varying cognitive abilities, developmental and learning disabilities, sensory impairments, and different cultural, linguistic, and socioeconomic backgrounds—in today's inclusive classrooms. It is based on the premise that children of differing abilities and backgrounds will benefit both academically and socially from cooperative learning.

In the process of conducting courses and workshops and providing consultation to educators on using cooperative learning to create inclusive classrooms over the last decade, we have noticed among teachers a growing recognition of the enormous potential of this method. It is hoped that the days of simplistic reactions to often poor implementation of cooperative learning ("I tried cooperative learning one Friday afternoon last month and it didn't work") are over. Educators are realizing that there is a lot more to structuring successful groups than simply putting students in a circle and telling them to cooperate. We know that in order for cooperative learning to be successful, certain conditions must be met, such as positive interdependence, individual accountability, and provisions for collaborative skill instruction and practice. Conversations with teachers and university students about cooperative learning are much more stimulating now, as we engage in dynamic discussions to analyze why groups of individuals succeed or struggle as they work together, whether the group goals are clear and attainable, whether the students possess the social skills to work together, whether the tasks are authentic and motivating, and whether all children are genuinely contributing to the group and accomplishing their individual goals.

This book focuses on how *all* children can flourish in one inclusive classroom—regardless of their individual ability levels, backgrounds, and learning styles; it is the outgrowth of a state-wide staff-development project to support general educators in their endeavors to create inclusive classrooms. Our goal is to provide teachers, teaching assistants, administrators, support personnel, families, community members and other professionals with suggestions for effectively implementing the cooperative learning approach in today's heterogeneous classrooms and schools. Guidelines are also provided to help educators, families, and other professionals work in cooperative teams. Throughout these pages you will encounter elements of the theoretical and empirical background of cooperative learning, as well as practical suggestions, case studies, illustrative examples, and lesson plans.

We hope this book is helpful to you. Its purpose is not to provide exhaustive coverage of cooperative learning—a rich literature already exists on this subject—rather, it focuses on how cooperative learning can be applied in instruction, behavior management, and the teaming of adults to assist in creating positive and productive classroom communities of diverse learners. If you discover that the ideas presented have relevance to you and you would like to share your ideas and experiences, please write us.

JoAnne W. Putnam, Ph.D.
Luanna H. Meyer, Ph.D.
Cheryl A. Utley, Ph.D.

REFERENCES

American Council on Education. (1988). *Minorities in higher education.* Seventh annual status report. Washington, DC: Author.

Cortés, C.E. (1981). The societal curriculum: Implications for multiethnic education. In J.A. Banks (Ed.), *Education in the 80's: Multiethnic education.* Washington, DC: National Education Association.

Nieto, S. (1992). *Affirming diversity: The sociopolitical context of multicultural education.* New York: Longman Publishing Co.

Foreword

An inclusive classroom setting is one in which the members recognize each other's individual differences and strive to support one another's efforts. In more traditional classroom arrangements, neither competition nor individual work promotes acceptance of differences; in heavy doses, in fact, they can actually prevent it. But diversity is celebrated within a cooperative context. And those who work and learn in a cooperative setting benefit from diversity, as it is the differences among members—differences in their talents, skills, perceptions, and thoughts—that make a cooperative group powerful. In fact, the weakest group that one could assemble would be one whose members were all alike, with the same perspectives, strengths, and limitations. A powerful group is one whose members' aggregate talents and ideas make it much more creative and adept at problemsolving than any individual could be alone; this is true of a cooperative learning group in the classroom, of a cooperative teaching team, and of a strong community or society.

The concept of celebrating diversity is of central importance to this book. However, differences within groups can initially cause difficulties. Few of us are used to explaining and elaborating on our ideas in terms that others can easily understand, or to listening intently and carefully considering others' ideas and perspectives. The key to the success of heterogeneous cooperative groups may well be the persistence of teachers who are determined to build a cooperative umbrella over a diverse group of students by teaching them the skills that they need to make inclusion work.

When teachers persist in changing classrooms into cooperative settings, a number of positive outcomes result:

1. The achievement levels of all students increase. Although the largest gains usually occur among students at the struggling, undermotivated end of the spectrum, there are clear achievement benefits for all students. For example, at the University of Minnesota, where the authors teach, Dr. Pat Heller has found that the most accomplished physics students achieve higher on problemsolving when they work cooperatively with others who are less able than themselves than they do when working alone.
2. Students tend to feel more positive about themselves and to be better psychologically adjusted when they are part of a group in a cooperative setting.
3. Students also accept differences more readily, both in and outside of the classroom. Cooperative efforts can help them outgrow their initial narrow stereotypes of one another and find out who each member of the team really is as they work toward a common goal and celebrate team efforts together.

It is important to keep in mind that there is a huge difference between simply putting students into groups and actually teaching them to care about one another's learning. One is just a seating arrangement, the other an interaction pattern. As is stated in more detail in the chapters that follow, there are five basic elements that must be present in order to foster a cooperative relationship: *positive independence, individual accountability, small-group skills, face-to-face interaction, and analysis of results.*

In order for teachers to successfully structure cooperative learning groups among students (or enter into them with other professionals) they must devote themselves to a serious study of what cooperation is and of what strategies are most effective for making it work. The authors would venture that it takes about 2 years of practice to integrate cooperative teaching and learning procedures into one's repertoire to the point where they are both natural and effective. This is best accomplished by teams of professionals who are themselves cooperative and determined. Very often, successful environments in which diversity is celebrated are built by teams of general and special educators and support personnel who themselves model the cooperation that they are encouraging among students. As educators, we need to develop our own celebration of diversity and define our own shared goals; we need to polish up our own cooperative skills at the same time that we are providing a powerful cooperative learning environment for students. Read this book, continue to work toward a cooperative classroom, and begin celebrating.

Roger T. Johnson, Ed.D.
Department of Curriculum and Instruction
University of Minnesota, Minneapolis

David W. Johnson, Ed.D.
Department of Educational Psychology
University of Minnesota, Minneapolis

Acknowledgments

This book is the work of many persons. I am grateful to the outstanding contributors who took precious time from their demanding professions to write the chapters; to Dr. Luanna Meyer for her encouragement and support in seeking publication of this manuscript; to Sylvia Rosen, Minneapolis, Minnesota, for her excellent editorial work; to Julie Morrison for typing part of the manuscript, and to the Rural Institute on Disabilities and the School of Education at the University of Montana for their support.

Thanks also to the Montana State Disabilities Planning and Advisory Council and the Bureau of Special Education, Office of Public Instruction, for their funding and support, which culminated in the project *Celebrating Diversity: Cooperative Learning and Strategies for Inclusion*. The chapters in this volume, with the exception of Chapters 2, 6, and 7, were developed for the *Celebrating Diversity* project under contract with the Montana State Disabilities Planning and Advisory Council (Contract #91-154-3490). These chapters have been expanded and updated with permission for this volume. The content does not necessarily reflect the position or policy of the Planning and Advisory Council or Bureau of Education and no official endorsement of these materials should be inferred.

Sarah Cheney, John Houseman Jr., Leslie Kahan, and the talented team of professionals at Paul H. Brookes Publishing Co. have provided tremendous assistance in the production of this book. Sarah Cheney's perspectives, professionalism, and cooperative skills have proven invaluable. John Houseman's skillful editing and perceptions have strengthened the book considerably. The staff of Brookes Publishing certainly deserves the fine reputation they have earned for their commitment to quality.

I especially want to thank the educators, families, and students who have influenced and enriched our understanding of cooperative learning. The royalties from the sale of this book are contributed to the Montana Developmental Disabilities Planning and Advisory Council to further their work in building inclusive classrooms and communities.

This book is dedicated to the Montana teachers who work in schools spread across vast expanses, yet form a cohesive community on behalf of children with diverse abilities.

Cooperative Learning and Strategies for Inclusion

1

The Movement Toward Teaching and Learning in Inclusive Classrooms

JoAnne W. Putnam

American education is on the verge of tremendous change. A new generation of educators is taking its place in our schools, and the challenges they face are greater than ever before. Government, business, and industrial leaders worry that American schools are no longer competitive with those in other countries, that they are not turning out enough mathematicians and scientists for the needs of the twenty-first century, and that the country is losing its international preeminence. At the same time, schools are hampered by insufficient funding, the overburdening of teachers, and the persistence of outdated concepts that still govern the education of many public school students.

Most of us recognize that the mission of schools is evolving, but the direction of this change is still uncertain. American education is in an era of transition as we strive to ensure high academic standards while at the same time educating all students. Schools are being asked to assume ever-expanding roles, to address societal problems ranging from violence, drug abuse, and poverty, to discrimination (Pipho, 1992). The goal of education has also shifted from preparing students to enter an economy based on manufacturing to the preparation of individuals who can function in a highly technological, service-oriented, and mobile society. What is certain is that our educational system must be responsive to the increasing rate of change in society.

CHALLENGES IN AMERICAN EDUCATION

Changing Student Populations

Hodgkinson (1991) described the spectacular shifts that have occurred since the 1980s in the nature of the children who come to school, and specifically in the growing number of students who, due to a lack of resources in their homes and communities, are unlikely to succeed in today's schools. One-third of American children are at risk for school failure. These children are an average of 2 years behind their grade level in the 6th grade and 4 years behind by the 12th grade. Before these children even enter kindergarten, they are at risk, as most of them come from minority and immigrant populations in which English is a second language and poverty is widespread. American schools are now characterized by cultural and ethnic diversity, and minority populations continue to grow rapidly. Between 1980 and 1990, the white population increased 8%, while the African American population grew 16%, the Asian population 65%, and the Hispanic population 44%. In many areas of the country, particularly large cities, "minorities" are quickly becoming the majority. Today, students come to school from many different backgrounds, with different traditions and languages.

Since 1987, one-fourth of all preschool children have been living in poverty. Annually, about 350,000 children are born to mothers addicted to cocaine. The "Norman Rockwell" family, with a working father, a housewife mother, and two school-age children now accounts for only 6% of U.S. households. It is estimated that on any given night, between 50,000 and 200,000 children are homeless (Hodgkinson, 1991).

The composition of the typical American classroom is also changing with respect to the number of students with disabilities who are being served. Currently, at least 68.6% of students requiring special education services are attending inclusive classes for part (40% or more) or all of the school day. Between the 1987–1988 and 1988–1989 school years, the rate of inclusive-class placement for students with disabilities rose 1.6% (U.S. Department of Education, 1991). This trend is predicted to continue; in the future, ever-greater numbers of students will receive their education in the mainstream. Indeed, an increasing number of school districts are providing instruction in inclusive classrooms for nearly all students with disabilities (see Villa & Thousand, chap. 4, this volume, and Jakupcak, chap. 8, this volume). In these districts, the few exceptions to inclusive placement involve students with severe emotional disturbance or behavioral problems, or those with complex medical needs, as these students usually require frequent and intensive psychological or medical therapy or intervention.

Our old assumptions about students and their families no longer apply. Changes in the school population dictate that teachers be prepared to deal with a greater diversity of students and social problems than they have in the past:

> In spite of a rapidly changing student population our system of education has not changed appreciably, and this is part of the problem. We haven't gotten worse, we simply haven't been able to keep up with the changes that have come about in the population of clients with whom we deal. Clearly our education system is on the front line in attempting to deal with the crisis. (Robson, personal communication, November, 1992)

Poor Achievement and Failing Instructional Practices

Even though our population of students and the goals of American education are changing, our instructional approaches have been slow to evolve. Public schools have received harsh criticism since the 1980s for failing to produce students who achieve proficiency in the basic subjects and, more recently, for falling behind in international comparisons (Stevenson & Stigler, 1992). Reports such as *A Nation at Risk,* by the National Commission on Excellence in Education (1983), recommend that schools place more emphasis on science, math, and writing; assign more homework to students; and extend the school year. Curiously, *A Nation at Risk* does not include discussion of students who are disabled and in need of special education services (Lipsky & Gartner, 1989).

Glasser (1986) criticized the commission's recommendations, referring to them as the "work 'em harder" approach, ill-suited to meeting the needs of the least motivated students in our schools—those children at risk for school failure and dropout. According to Glasser, one major deterrent to motivation and learning among students is an academic curriculum that lacks quality.

Goodlad's (1983) in-depth study of 1,016 schools identified several problems in American education: 1) a predominance of whole-class instruction, with very little instructional variability; 2) little emphasis on providing corrective feedback with guidance to students or on stimulating concept formation; 3) affectless (neither positive nor negative) classrooms; and 4) minimal teacher–student and student–student interaction (mostly lectures and monitored seatwork).

While observing student teachers in high schools, I have made a practice of peering in classroom windows when I walk down the hallways—my own informal survey of teacher–student and student–student interaction. With few exceptions, I have found the teacher in the front of the classroom, lecturing to the whole class or working at his or her desk. The students were either listening to a teacher lecture, responding to questions, or working quietly at their desks with books and other materials. There is, of course, a place for lecture and discussion in our classrooms, but over-reliance on this instructional model has been widely criticized. Many experts advocate encouraging students to become more actively engaged in designing their own learning experiences. Unfortunately, familiar ways are slow to change in American education.

Sorting and Tracking of Students

The traditional practice of placing students in different tracks, or homogeneous groups, to receive instruction is now subject to much debate (Oakes, 1985). During the 1980s, research has shown that tracking and ability-grouped class assignments negatively influence most children's school opportunities and outcomes (Oakes & Lipton, 1992). Tracking has been criticized on the basis of instructional, as well as ethical, concerns. Research suggests that "grouping and tracking do not increase overall achievement in schools but they do produce inequity" (Gamoran, 1991, p. 11). While the national debate continues, many schools are moving toward alternatives to tracking. The National Education Association has resolved that tracking as a practice should be eliminated (Oakes & Lipton, 1992).

The "Commission on Chapter One," a 28-member group of school officials, child advocates, and business executives, was convened to study the effectiveness of federally funded Chapter 1 "pull-out" remedial programs (Jordan, 1992). The Commission has found such programs to be discriminatory and not as effective as heterogeneous classroom programs. They have called for an end to pull-out practices and recommend keeping the children who need remedial help with the typical students all day. Pull-out practices socially stigmatize lower-income students and put them at an academic disadvantage because they are taught only the most basic skills. The Commission proposed funnelling the money used for Chapter 1 services away from individual tutoring and into whole-class resources, recommending that for each class with 10 children below the poverty line, the teacher receive an additional $9,000 for extra materials, aides, teacher training, or other needs.

The differential schooling provided to secondary students on the basis of whether they are bound for the workforce or for college may not be justified given current economic conditions. Today, a foodservice worker or auto mechanic must learn to use highly technical equipment and to compensate should that equipment fail. Brandt (1992) suggests that the aims of college and work preparation programs are not mutually exclusive, and that the system should require higher educational standards for all students.

Rochester Schools' Superintendent Peter McWalters aptly characterized the American education system as the *grim sorter*: "If we start out with 100 students, eventually we'll sort them out into groups and categories and we'll end up with two kids in a room," he observes, "and then we'll ask for help with one of them" (Buckley, 1989, p. 61).

THE RATIONALE FOR INCLUSIVE CLASSROOMS

Past failures in serving students with disabilities have occurred for a variety of reasons. Over the years, piecemeal and token changes in the educational treatment of children with disabilities have occurred through the adaptation or expansion of existing models, rather than through the development of distinctly different or innovative ones. For example, when PL 94-142 called for placement in the least restrictive environment, educators were selective about which children were moved into general classrooms. Multidisciplinary teams were able to decide what constituted the "least restrictive environment" for each particular student. The choice was often a special classroom or resource room where instruction was "specialized" to fit the needs of atypical students. The philosophy of educating children with disabilities was that these children had to be treated differently. If the standard approach of the general classroom was not working, then educators simply moved the child out, rather than attempting to adapt the standard techniques to the child's unique learning requirements. Unfortunately, to a large extent, this philosophy of differential treatment and removal still prevails today.

But researchers have not been able to prove that pulling students out of classrooms for special education services produces significant benefits (Lipsky & Gartner, 1989). Numerous review and efficacy studies have compared special education pull-out programs with general class placement and have found that, for the most part, there are few, if any, positive effects for students at any level of ability who are placed in special education settings (see Lipsky & Gartner, 1989; Meyer & Putnam, 1988, for discussions of this research). Weiner (1985) reviewed 50 studies that compared the academic performance of students with mild disabilities placed in either mainstream classrooms or segregated settings. The integrated group's mean academic performance was in the 80th percentile, while segregated students scored in the 50th percentile. Semmel, Gottlieb, and Robinson's (1979) review of the efficacy literature found that "there is an absence of a conclusive body of evidence which confirms that special education services appreciably enhance the academic and/or social accomplishments of handicapped children beyond what can be expected without special education" (p. 267).

Civil Rights and Moral Imperative

The most compelling rationale for integration is based on cultural values and human rights. The civil rights movement used the legislative mandate of the 1954 *Brown v. Board of Education* decision in the fight to eliminate the negative effects of political, social, and educational segregation. Today, advocates are fighting against another insidious form of segregation—the denial of equal opportunities to students who happen to have a disability, are from a different cultural/language background, or sometimes display behavior problems:

> If we want an integrated society in which all persons are considered of equal worth and as having equal rights, segregation in the schools cannot be justified. That is, no defensible excuses or rationales can be offered, and no amount of scientific research can be conducted that will in the final analysis justify segregation. Segregation has no justification; it is simply unfair and morally wrong to segregate any students, including those defined as disabled, from the mainstream of regular education. (Stainback, Stainback, & Forest, 1989, p.4)

According to the Fourteenth Amendment to the Constitution, people are equal under the law and, thus, deserve equal opportunities in our schools. Such philosophical absolutes in a democratic society lead us to the conclusion that segregation and ability grouping are unethical, if not unconstitutional.

Now, many school districts are examining the appropriateness of their compartmentalized and fragmented services for students with disabilities or learning problems. Some districts have arrived at the conclusion that an integrated, or merged, service delivery system is the most effective and equitable for all students (Fink, 1992).

Given the lack of evidence that special education programs are academically better than inclusive class placement for students, should we —can we—continue to defend this form of segregation and the social and psychological disadvantages that it entails?

The Importance of Access to the Core Curriculum

Educators are becoming increasingly aware of the many deleterious effects of not giving all children the opportunity to experience the core curriculum of a school district: children's self-esteem and motivation are diminished; they have fewer opportunities for observational learning from peer models; and they are very likely to fall further and further behind in academics, which often precludes their ever returning to regular classes (The Council of Great City Schools, 1986). Being pulled out from core-curriculum classes often has a negative effect on self-esteem because students feel singled out as being different or less intelligent, and this can cause them to be targeted for labeling by peers as "special education" or "remedial" students. The negative effects of labeling and stigmatization associated with pull-out special education programs have long been a topic of discussion in the literature (Heward & Orlansky, 1992).

Furthermore, in trying to improve a child's skills in those areas of study in which he or she is having difficulties, pull-out programs can sometimes fail to take the child's own strengths and preferences into account. For example, the parents of one child with a learning disability complained to me that for 3 years their son had been pulled out of science class to receive special education in math. What is unfortunate about this situation is that science is actually this student's favorite subject and area of greatest strength.

Some special education or remedial pull-out programs offer a curriculum that is inferior to that presented in typical classes, both in *quantity*, or how much time is spent actively engaged in instruction (Ysseldyke, 1984), and *quality*, which refers to how differentiated the instruction is, how well suited it is to the individual needs of the student. Remedial and resource pull-out programs have been found to have little coherence with the various instructional activities experienced in the general classroom. A study by Allington and McGill-Franzen (1989) found a great deal of fragmentation of curricular experiences in both remedial and resource-room reading programs. "Not only did these students have to deal with unrelated reading activities in the classroom, but they were also assigned additional sets of unrelated activities and tasks in the support settings" (p. 84).

It is antithetical to the intent of the Individuals with Disabilities Education Act (IDEA) that students classified as disabled should be further disadvantaged by receiving special education interventions in separate settings. The fact that students who are removed from general classes for instruction are known to fall further and further behind their peers in the general class should sound the alarm for both general and special educators. A survey of students placed in special education classrooms in Pittsburgh indicated that only 1.4% of those students ever returned to general education settings, and this statistic is considered to be about average for large cities in the nation (Lipsky & Gartner, 1989).

Criticisms of curricular approaches are not limited to pull-out or remedial programs, and they have been leveled on behalf of children both with and without disabilities, including those labeled as gifted. These criticisms were reviewed by Knoll and Meyer (1987), who argued for increased efforts to adapt the general school curricula and provide individualized assistance to all children, rather than maintain separate, specialized environments for each of the various groupings.

Schools should consider adopting more-flexible scheduling arrangements that allow all students to participate in the core curriculum at specified times. Then, a portion of the day could be designated for student "choice" and "tutorial" activities. For example, during the afternoon students could elect to participate in one of a number of activities, such as a unit on sign language, a multimedia computer skills class, or an art class. Time would also be available for *all* students during the afternoon for any necessary tutorials or individualized activities that did not lend themselves to the core-curriculum time. Different activities would take place in different areas of the school, and students would not be assigned to locations according to ability levels (e.g., a resource room). Students with special talents and abilities could pursue their interests with community mentors, through library work, by engaging in a cooperative activity, or by taking a satellite course. A student with an avid interest in wild flowers might work with an expert from the local garden club or college in pursuing applied research and study. If this same student happened to have difficulties in the area of math, he or she could also work with a highly talented math teacher and a peer during part of the "choice" period. Better yet, the botanist mentor and the math teacher could find ways to integrate mathematics into a creative cooperative-group botany project involving data collection, sampling, and quantifying plant communities utilizing various mathematical concepts and operations.

The Social Impact of Inclusion

Researchers and practitioners are beginning to recognize the critical impact of social ecology—of the characteristics of the environment—on children's behavior and learning outcomes. Learning itself is a social act; it is more closely related to the processes of socialization than to simple instruction (Resnick, 1990). The "remedial" model of special education —providing education in segregated settings—does not adequately address the social-interaction and learning deficits of children with disabilities; indeed, it may do more to perpetuate these deficits than to improve them, especially if the effects of the social environment are not taken into account. For students who exhibit social-skill and learning deficits, the environmental opportunities made available to them are critical to the remediation of those deficits.

Pulling together students with problems in the same class for instruction limits critical opportunities for developing social competence and may, in some cases, reinforce problem behaviors. It is important that atypical students observe a range of behaviors, not just those of students who are challenged academically or socially. Inclusive class settings have proven to be advantageous because they allow students to observe socially and culturally acceptable models for learning appropriate behavior. True friendships and support systems rarely develop when students are physically or socially separated from peers or other members of the community; segregating students for instruction limits possibilities for friendships to form between individuals of varying abilities (Meyer & Putnam, 1988). Such friendships and acquaintances are the foundation for a life-long support system for many people. Typical students who get to know peers with disabilities are often motivated to become their friends, good neighbors, and even future employers (Meyer, 1985).

TEACHERS' CONCERNS

Teachers who for the first time face the prospect of serving students with disabilities or students from different cultural or ethnic backgrounds may question whether they are willing or even able to take on such challenges.

Many teachers feel that they have insufficient training in methods of adapting instruction to such students. They find it difficult to imagine breaking out of the mold of traditional teaching approaches. To some, whole-class lecture and discussion, including the teacher's role as the "sage on the stage," is a good model simply because it has such a long history and has worked for them in the past.

Sometimes teachers who do try to work with students with diverse needs are distressed by their feelings of inadequacy and are reluctant to try again, and these teachers are perhaps the most reluctant to accept help or training when it is offered. Searl, Ferguson, and Biklen (1985) observed that teachers who had a record of willingness to experiment and to be involved in change were the most likely to take advantage of training and consultation when they were made available.

Teachers often ask the following questions about including students who have previously been pulled out of regular classes or segregated for instruction:

Do inclusion programs really work? How do they operate?

My teacher education program did not prepare me to teach children with diverse abilities. How do I teach them?

When I have children with diverse abilities in my classroom, will I be forced to short-change my typical students?

Are there reasonable adaptations that I can make?

What help will I get in teaching these students?

Is it all right to vary my achievement expectations for these students?

Will I need more training?

Where will the money for extra technology or teacher assistants come from?

Will I get extra pay or fewer students?

These are legitimate questions. They deserve thoughtful consideration and action. In St. Paul, Minnesota, a survey of students receiving special education services, their parents, teachers, administrators, and support staff disclosed that class size and teacher workload were the major concerns of all respondents (St. Paul Public Schools, 1984). Respondents indicated that although special educators were the most knowledgeable, supportive, and interested in mainstreaming, the bulk of the responsibility for mainstreaming actually fell on general education teachers. General educators were also concerned about possible negative effects on typical students and the need for inservice training to help them feel more prepared. They considered their own attitudes to be of little importance to the success of special students. Special educators, however, felt that general classroom teachers' attitudes were critical to special education students' success. The survey also pointed to the importance of staff members of a school, and even of a school system, sharing their knowledge in order to make mainstream programs work.

Let's admit it: it is not always easy for teachers to instruct students with widely differing ability levels and learning styles in the same classroom. Students who require special attention and services do not always work at the same pace or have the same educational objectives and curricula as their age-peers. Unfortunately, the past practice of structuring individualized learning activities and tutorials for atypical students often resulted in "islands in the mainstream"—students who were isolated from their peers and excluded from the ongoing class curriculum (Biklen, 1985, p. 18). It only seems fair that teachers who are asked to educate students with differing abilities receive adequate preparation, special support and services, the commitment of the administration, and opportunities to engage in a positive team approach.

BREAKING WITH THE PAST

Historically, the aims of separate placement were to shield students from the social rejection that they sometimes experienced in general classes and to provide specialized instruction to address their unique learning needs. In fact, one reason for the initial establishment of special classes for students with disabilities in the 1950s and 1960s was to "protect" them from the neglect or rejection that they sometimes encountered in general classes, as well as to provide them with what was supposed to be more systematic, intensive instruction. General classes did not meet the needs of these students, but this was partly because no one expected them to.

Another reason for segregating students with disabilities was—and is—the assumption that they learn in different ways than "normal" persons do. Professionals once believed that separate psychological theories and techniques were required to educate students with disabilities. For example, one psychologist held that the brains of persons with mental retardation were less "permeable" than those of people without mental retardation. Universities and colleges offered courses in theories of mental retardation and learning disabilities, and it was assumed that people who were specially prepared to work with children with disabilities should not work with typical children, and vice versa. But Sarason and Doris (1978) argued forcefully against the belief that separate theories and psychological principles should be applied to persons with disabilities, maintaining that just because people develop differently does not mean they are governed by entirely different psychological processes. Diversity among people should not be equated with a diversity of principles underlying human behavior. It is interesting to note that many of the instructional and behavior approaches once developed for students with disabilities, such as learning strategies, meta-cognitive strategies, or behavior-change strategies (e.g., behavior contracts, token economies) are now applied in the mainstream of education because they seem to work with a broad population of children.

Today, school personnel are being urged to develop educational programs that will serve a diversity of students and maximize the socio-emotional development and increase the learning capacity of all children. Is it possible to achieve these goals? This volume attempts to address this question by elaborating on cooperative learning and cooperative teaching as promising avenues for future practice. An underlying assumption is that in today's heterogeneous classrooms and schools, the goals of public education are most likely to be attained by teaching children to work and to learn together, that is, by adopting cooperative learning techniques in classrooms and encouraging the cooperation and teaming of teachers, parents, and others (Johnson & Johnson, 1989; Slavin, 1990). This volume also stresses the importance of taking into account the unique needs, characteristics, and learning styles of all students in the design and delivery of instruction. Actually, the concept of "special education," was initially formulated to address the *individual* needs of atypical students, but we recognize now that all students, and not just students with disabilities, differ from one another in some ways. Those of us who have worked in the field of special education for a number of years have encountered numerous students who "don't fit" into the education system. We now realize that some students without disabilities also "don't fit" into the traditional system, whether it is because they are unmotivated, gifted, have been socialized in repressive ways, or simply cannot sit at a desk for long periods of time. Hopefully, we will find a way to develop efficient and effective individualized educational programs for all students, and not just those identified as needing special education services.

CONCLUDING COMMENTS

To blend students with challenging learning and social needs into today's classrooms, we must create climates that avoid isolation, rejection, and stereotyping. Cooperative learning offers an alternative to "islands in the mainstream"—students with special needs who remain isolated despite being placed in the general education classroom—by engaging students of various ability levels in shared instructional activities and learning experiences (Johnson, Johnson, & Holubec, 1986). Students with differences—even students who are highly gifted—are less likely to be rejected when their classmates get to know their strengths as well as their weaknesses and when all students experience the satisfaction of helping one another to reach their mutual goals (Johnson & Johnson, 1989).

A full-blown restructuring is needed to meet the challenge of diversity in our schools. Lessons have been learned from special education that are also applicable to general education. Instructional techniques and strategies that could be beneficial to all students have been developed. It is time for special education to join forces with general education to transform our school environments—to encourage all students to live up to their capacities, realize their dreams, and find a place in our pluralistic world.

What does this mean for educators? We need to change the way we do things. Both "general" and "special" educators must assume new roles and responsibilities in schools. General education and special education programs should be merged in both our schools and universities. Our instructional methodologies must evolve. We really have no choice but to change.

One purpose of this volume, therefore, is to provide some practical "how to"s for educators who serve a diversity of students in inclusive classrooms. A second purpose is to encourage a "can do" attitude among educators, families, and community members in meeting today's educational challenges. Our belief is that cooperative learning, to be used most effectively, should be applied at all levels of the educational ecosystem; including cooperative groups of learners, cooperation and teaming among teachers, and cooperation with families and the broader community. Although this volume focuses specifically on a cooperative learning approach, there are other useful, highly compatible forms of instruction. Cooperative learning should not be seen as a panacea for solving all the problems of our schools, but it is a sound technique for structuring a responsive education community.

REFERENCES

Allington, R.L., & McGill-Franzen, A. (1989). Different programs, indifferent instruction. In D.K. Lipsky and A. Gartner (Eds.), *Beyond separate education: Quality education for all* (pp. 75–97). Baltimore: Paul H. Brookes Publishing Co.
Biklen, D. (1985). *Achieving the complete school: Strategies for effective mainstreaming.* New York: Teachers' College Press.

Brandt, R. (1992). Reconsidering our commitments. *Educational Leadership, 50*(2), 5.

Buckley, J. (1989, March 13). Fixing the teaching, not the kids: Reversing the trend in special education in Rochester. *U.S. News & World Report*, pp. 61–62.

The Council of Great City Schools. (1986). *Special education: Views from America's cities*. Washington, DC: Author.

Education for All Handicapped Children Act of 1975, PL 94-142. (August 23, 1977). Title 20, U.S.C. 1401 et seq: *U.S. Statutes at Large, 89*, 773–796.

Fink, S. (1992). How we restructured our categorical programs. *Educational Leadership, 50*(2), 42–43.

Gamoran, A. (1991). Is ability grouping equitable? *Educational Leadership, 50*(2), 11–17.

Glasser, W.J. (1986). *Control theory in the classroom*. New York: Harper and Row.

Goodlad, J. (1983). A study of schooling: Some findings and hypotheses. *Phi Delta Kappan, 64*, 462–470.

Heward, W.L., & Orlansky, M.D. (1992). *Exceptional children* (4th ed.). New York: Merill Publishing Company.

Hodgkinson, H. (1991). Reform versus reality. *Phi Delta Kappan, 73*(1), 8–16.

Individuals with Disabilities Education Act of 1990 (IDEA), PL 101–476. (October 30, 1990). Title 20, U.S.C. 1400 et seq: *U.S. Statutes at Large, 105*, 587–608.

Johnson, D.W., & Johnson, R.T. (1989). *Cooperation and competition: Theory and research*. Edina, MN: Interaction Books.

Johnson, D.W., Johnson, R.T., & Holubec, E.J. (1986). *Circles of learning: Cooperation in the classroom* (rev. ed.). Edina, MN: Interaction Books.

Jordan, M. (1992, December 11). Program cheats poor children, report asserts. *Anchorage Daily News*, p. A3.

Knoll, J., & Meyer, L.H. (1987). Integrated schooling and educational quality: Principles and effective practices. In M. Berres & P. Knoblock (Eds.), *Managerial models of mainstreaming* (pp. 41–59). Rockville, MD: Aspen.

Lipsky, D.K., & Gartner, A. (Eds.). (1989). *Beyond separate education: Quality education for all*. Baltimore: Paul H. Brookes Publishing Co.

Meyer, L.H. (1985, December). *Why integration, or why nonhandicapped kids should be friends and not tutors*. Paper presented at the 12th Annual Conference of the Association for Persons with Severe Handicaps, Boston.

Meyer, L.H., & Putnam, J.W. (1988). Social integration. In V.B. Van Hasselt, P.S. Strain, & M. Hersen (Eds.), *Handbook of developmental and physical disabilities* (pp. 107–133). Elmsford, NY: Pergamon Press.

National Commission on Excellence in Education. (1983). *A nation at risk: The imperative for educational reform*. Washington, DC: U.S. Government Printing Office.

Oakes, J. (1985). *Keeping track: How schools structure inequality*. New Haven, CT: Yale University Press.

Oakes, J., & Lipton, M. (1992). Detracking schools: Early lessons from the field. *Phi Delta Kappan, 73*(6), 448–454.

Pipho, C. (1992). Caught between competing visions. *Phi Delta Kappan, 74*(2), 102–103.

Resnick, L. (1990). Literacy in school and out. *Dedalus, 119*(2), 169–185.

Sarason, S., & Doris, J. (1978). Mainstreaming: Dilemmas, opposition, opportunities. In M.C. Reynolds (Ed.), *Futures of education for exceptional students: Emerging structures* (pp. 3–40). Reston, VA: The Council for Exceptional Children.

Searl, S.J., Ferguson, D.L., & Biklen, D. (1985). The front line . . . teachers. In D. Biklen (Ed.), *Achieving the complete school: Strategies for effective mainstreaming* (pp. 52–103). New York: Teachers' College Press.

Semmel, M.I., Gottlieb, J., & Robinson, N.M. (1979). Mainstreaming: Perspectives on educating handicapped children in the public schools. In D. Berliner (Ed.), *Review of research in education* (Vol. 7, pp. 223–279). Washington, DC: American Educational Research Association.

Slavin, R.E. (1990). *Cooperative learning: Theory, research and practice.* Englewood Cliffs, NJ: Prentice Hall.

St. Paul Public Schools. (1984). *Special Education Council Mainstreaming Study.* (ERIC Document Reproduction Service No. 268753).

Stainback, S., Stainback, W., & Forest, M. (Eds.). (1989). *Educating all students in the mainstream of regular education.* Baltimore: Paul H. Brookes Publishing Co.

Stevenson, H., & Stigler, J. (1992). *The learning gap.* New York: Summit Books.

U.S. Department of Education. (1991). *Thirteenth annual report to Congress on the Implementation of the Individuals with Disabilities Education Act.* Washington, DC: U.S. Government Printing Office.

Weiner, R. (1985). *PL 94-142: Impact on the schools.* Washington, DC: Capitol Publications.

Ysseldyke, J.E., Thurlow, M.L., Mecklenburg, C., & Garden, J. (1984). Opportunity to learn for regular and special education students during reading instruction. *Remedial and Special Education, 5,* 29–37.

2

The Process of
Cooperative Learning

JoAnne W. Putnam

The process of implementing cooperative learning requires modifications in the way that teachers organize and manage their classrooms. Although the transition from traditional whole-class instruction to a cooperative model may not be easy, it is a golden investment in the future for a diversity of students and teachers. The current movement away from tracking and toward inclusive classrooms must be linked with appropriate modifications in teaching techniques in order to preempt the breakdown in learning and morale that can sometimes result when classroom demographics begin to change and instructional methods remain static.

Extensive research has shown that cooperative learning groups promote high achievement and positive interpersonal outcomes, but only under certain conditions (Johnson & Johnson, 1989; Slavin, 1990). Unfortunately, the numerous potential benefits of cooperative learning are not always realized in our classrooms, due to poor or partial implementation or infrequent use (Joyce, 1992). Educators are not commonly aware of the conditions that are essential for cooperative learning to lead to positive outcomes; simply placing students in groups and asking them to cooperate will not ensure higher achievement or positive interpersonal outcomes.

Cooperative learning is a complex process, and many factors can determine its success or failure. Being a good math teacher entails more than a workshop in teaching math; it requires an entire program of study. Similarly, the complex processes that make up cooperative learning cannot be mastered in a 3-hour workshop. Educators need to understand what factors lead to successful group work, and they need to be able to analyze why groups sometimes fail. It may take 2 or 3 years of using the procedures and sharing successes and failures with colleagues before a teacher feels really comfortable with cooperative learning. Problems are likely to arise when teachers have not been adequately exposed to cooperative learning in their teacher-preparation programs or through inservice training. Additionally, teachers sometimes face barriers such as organizational constraints or a lack of support in their schools.

This chapter describes cooperative learning principles and identifies the conditions under which cooperative learning leads to enhanced student outcomes in the areas of academic achievement, peer relations, and self-esteem. Four major approaches to cooperative learning are described: the conceptual approach, the curricular approach, the structural approach, and complex instruction. It is assumed that cooperative learning should be used in conjunction with effective instructional strategies that take into account the individual needs and learning styles of each student. This is not the only way to organize instruction, but it is critical to providing a context in which students of various abilities and characteristics can support and learn with and from one another.

WHAT DISTINGUISHES COOPERATIVE LEARNING FROM TRADITIONAL GROUP INSTRUCTION?

In cooperative learning groups, individuals work together to reach common goals. Cooperative situations are often contrasted with individualistic situations, in which students work on their own and there is no correlation among their goal attainments (i.e., your performance on the spelling test does not affect mine, and vice versa), or with competitive situations, in which students try to outperform one another and their goal attainments are negatively correlated (i.e., if *you* are the top speller in the class, then *I* can't be). Although American educators have historically used group work in the classroom, they have not structured groups according to the principles of cooperative learning set forth by Johnson and Johnson (1989) and Slavin (1990). The following discussion identifies the basic characteristics and requirements that distinguish cooperative learning from traditional group instruction.

Positive Interdependence

During cooperative learning activities, the accomplishment of the group goal should depend on all members working together and coordinating their actions. It is important that students be concerned about the performance of all the group members. Students should not feel successful until each member of the group has attained both the group learning goal and his or her individual learning goal(s). This may require that students tutor one another and check on one another's progress.

Positive interdependence is the essence of cooperative learning—it is achieved when students think in terms of "we instead of me" (Johnson, Johnson, & Holubec, 1990). Among the methods for achieving positive interdependence are: 1) goal interdependence (a mutual goal or goals for the whole team); 2) task interdependence (division of labor); 3) resource interdependence (division and/or sharing of materials, resources, and information among individual group members); 4) role interdependence (assigning various roles to students); and 5) reward interdependence (giving a group reward for achieving the goal or goals).

Individual Accountability

All students should be held individually responsible for learning the material and contributing to the group. Insisting on individual accountability discourages "coasting" or "hitchhiking," in which one or a few of the students do the bulk of the work and the others take a free ride. Individual evaluations are essential in determining whether each student has mastered the material. Teachers can test each student individually or randomly select a student from each group to respond to questions or demonstrate or explain the material to the class. Students should also be encouraged to monitor themselves by periodically filling out an individual accountability evaluation form like the one shown in Figure 1.

Cooperative Skills

Students should be required to practice social and cooperative skills within their groups. Cooperative skills are those social skills commonly used in group activities. After determining what skills are needed by students, teachers should provide social-skill instruction by defining the skill, explaining its importance, demonstrating the skill, setting up practice situations in the groups, and giving students feedback on how well they are using the skill.

The particular skills taught will vary according to the age level of the students and the perceived need for specific social/cooperative skills. For example, some of the skills taught in elementary grades are staying with the group, sharing materials, taking turns, encouraging one another, and speaking in quiet voices. Secondary students may need to work on skills such as active listening, paraphrasing what others are saying, giving compliments, encouraging others to contribute ideas, and resolving controversy without criticizing group members personally.

When teachers explain a cooperative skill, it is often helpful to generate a T-Chart with the students. The T-Chart is a visual device that

---

Individual Accountability
Self-Monitoring Form

Name _____   Group name _____

Date _____   Subject _____

Did I contribute to the group work today?   yes _____   no _____

How? _____

_____

Did I reach my own learning goal today?   yes _____   no _____

My learning goal was: _____

_____

_____

What I accomplished: _____

_____

_____

Is there anything that I could do to improve my accountability? _____

_____

_____

My future accountability goal is: _____

_____

_____

Figure 1.   Individual accountability self-monitoring form.

shows children examples of the words, phrases, and body language that tend to be associated with a particular cooperative skill (Johnson et al., 1990). A sample T-Chart generated with student input is shown in Table 1.

Face-to-Face Interaction

Students should interact directly with one another while they are working. They may communicate verbally and/or nonverbally. Interaction should take place among students, rather than between students and ma-

Table 1. Social skills T-chart generated with the input of a 5th-grade class

Social skill: praising others

Sounds like	Looks like
Good job	Smiling
Fantastic	Thumbs up
Yes!	High-five
I like your idea	Leaning forward
Wicked good	Pat on the back
Super	Nodding head

terials or machines. When students are asked to work independently on a set of problems and then meet in groups to discuss the answers, they are not really engaging in cooperative learning, but rather in "individualistic learning—with talking" (Johnson et al., 1990).

Student Reflection and Goal Setting

At the close of a cooperative activity or series of activities, students evaluate how well their group has functioned and whether their group goals were achieved. This task may be accomplished by students within their small groups, or by the whole class led by the teacher. Periodically, the groups should fill out simple evaluation forms that help in analyzing the group's strengths and weakness and in identifying group goals for the next week (see Figure 2). Teachers should also observe the groups, sometimes using an observation form to record occurrences of expected behaviors and later sharing the results of their observations with the students themselves.

A student can also serve as an observer for the group. Using an observation form, the student should record and tally designated behaviors. Students can benefit tremendously from engaging in reflective discussions and individual goal setting to improve their personal academic and social behaviors and those of the group. It is also important for students to congratulate themselves for those things that they do well within their groups.

Heterogeneous Groups

Teachers should strive for heterogeneity when assigning students to groups. Each group should contain a mixture of students with respect to cognitive-ability levels; social and behavioral skill levels; gender; cultural, racial, and language characteristics; and socioeconomic status. Of course, there are times when it is appropriate for students to work in homogeneous groups based on mutual interests (e.g., a group dedicated

---

Cooperative Group Reflection and Goal Setting

Group name: _____

Date: _____

	Needs Improvement	Good	Excellent

How well did our group:

1. Complete the task?   ____   ____   ____

2. Use the time wisely?   ____   ____   ____

3. Practice the social skill?   ____   ____   ____

What we did especially well: _____

_____

_____

What we need to improve on: _____

_____

_____

Future goal(s): _____

_____

_____

Figure 2. Cooperative group reflection and goal setting.

to writing about a particular topic such as salmon fishing or herb garden-
ing), for instruction in specific skills in a subject area (e.g., multiplying
fractions in mathematics), or for other specific purposes.

Equal Opportunity for Success

All students should have a chance to contribute to the success of the
group and to improve themselves. For students who experience learning
or behavioral difficulties, teachers should individualize the criteria for
success and adapt the expectations or task requirements in a manner
appropriate to the student's ability and needs. Some students will need

reduced requirements, some will work toward improving their previous performance (Slavin, 1990), and others may work toward unique, individualized criteria. Table 2 summarizes the major differences between cooperative groups and more-traditional learning groups.

Unsuccessful Groups

Most of us have participated in groupwork, and most of us can conjure up memories of group disasters. Often, when we try to determine what factors contributed to a cooperative-group disaster, we find that one or more of the basic requirements of cooperative learning was not fulfilled. Can you recall doing the bulk of the work for a group project in a college class just because you happened to volunteer to type the paper? Are you still upset because everyone received an A, even though you had done most of the work? What about when the school subcommittee convened to discuss curricular changes and one person dominated the entire process, insisting that his or her ideas be adopted? Have you ever been excluded from an educational group because the membership was all male or all female? There may be some special education teachers who remember the days when they were not invited to be on school committees because it was believed that the school-wide issues to be addressed would not pertain to teachers of students with special needs.

These situations violate the principles of positive interdependence, individual accountability, and the need for cooperative skills and heterogeneous groups, and they are less likely to occur in well-structured cooperative groups. However, even when all the criteria for a good cooperative group are fulfilled, there is no guarantee that the group interaction will be pleasant or that group work is the easiest way to get things done. Cooperation doesn't happen automatically—it takes time and hard work.

Table 2. Differences between cooperative learning groups and traditional groups

Cooperative learning groups	Traditional learning groups
Positive interdependence	No positive interdependence
Individual accountability	No individual accountability
Cooperative skills taught directly	No cooperative skill instruction
Shared leadership	Appointed leader
Responsibility for success of all group members	Responsibility for one's own contribution
Teacher observation and feedback	Teacher withdraws from groups
Equal opportunity for success	Uniform standard for success
Groups review process and set goals for future	No review or goal setting

Adapted from Johnson, Johnson, and Holubec (1990).

Today's ineffectual group might be tomorrow's triumphant group if the members are willing to engage in reflective problem solving, to strive to do things differently, and to simply persevere in reaching for their goals.

LESSON PLAN:
A cooperative unit on endangered species

Ms. Wright's 5th-grade class is studying endangered species. She has planned an interdisciplinary thematic unit that incorporates science, art, and writing. The students are assigned to work in cooperative learning groups of four to study an endangered species of their own choice, to write a paper with illustrations, and to make a group presentation to the class. The students will also contact the Nature Conservancy to learn about the species (both endangered and nonendangered) native to the local area.

Lesson objectives: To research an endangered species, write a group paper on that species, contact conservation organizations about animal species native to the local area, and give a class presentation.
Time allotted: About 1 period a day for 3 weeks.
Materials: Reference materials about endangered species; computers and discs; Hypercard program; art paper, pens, markers, and colored pencils.
Roles: peer editors (2), illustrator, project manager
Heterogeneous groups: Students are assigned to groups of four. Ms. Wright uses her knowledge of the students to assign students of various ability levels to each group. For example, Steven, who has autism, is assigned to a group with two students of average ability and a high-achieving student. The groups are also mixed with respect to gender, cultural and ethnic background, and interpersonal skill levels.

(continued)

Positive interdependence: Each group will select an endangered species to study and report on (goal interdependence). The individual students in each group will choose one aspect of the endangered species to study and write about. For example, one group has chosen the Komodo Dragon of Indonesia as their endangered species, and another has chosen Beluga whales. Individual group members have each decided to write about one aspect of the topic, such as description and characteristics, habitat, geographic range, and factors that threaten the species (task interdependence). The members of each group will combine their contributions into one paper, each writing their sections on the computer in the classroom (material interdependence). Two group members will serve as peer editors for the group, a manager will coordinate the various aspects of the project, and an artist will provide illustrations (role interdependence). Then, a group presentation will be made to the class. The group will contact the local agencies to learn about reptiles or whales in their own area. Students will receive a group grade on their paper (reward interdependence), as well as individual grades for their own contributions.

Individual accountability: Individual students will each be graded on the section that they contribute to the group project. Each student will be individually tested with an essay test at the end of the unit. Individual contributions to the group (e.g., participation, effort, organization) will also be rated by group members on a form provided by the teacher.

Criteria for success: Successful completion of a high-quality group paper with individual contributions, a class presentation, and a unit test.

Cooperative skills: The cooperative skill designated for this unit is encouraging others to participate. The skill is taught directly to the students by the teacher. Students will be formally observed by the teacher, who will use an observation form. The teacher will provide feedback to the students.

Adaptations for individual differences: The artists for the groups are self-selected. In the Komodo Dragon group, Steven, who has autism, has artistic talent and has volunteered to do the illustrations for the group. His predominant mode of communication is facilitated communication with a laptop computer, so his facilitator (teaching assistant) is present when he communicates. Although Steven is essentially nonverbal, he is able to type his section of the paper using the computer. His work benefits from peer editing, as do the other students' contributions. For the group presentation, Steven will create a multimedia presentation using the Macintosh computer in his classroom. With the help of a student from the local high school, he has created a Hypercard stack on his topic that incorporates print, graphics, and sound.

Steven is working on the social skill of staying with the group, as his previous experience with group work is minimal and he is inclined to physically remove himself from activities and retreat into himself. Steven's grading criteria has been adapted based on his individualized learning objectives. He is able to take the unit test using facilitated communication, but his criteria for success is 75%, whereas the other students are expected to attain 80% mastery.

Evaluation and Student Reflection: The teacher will monitor the groups by observing and recording students' practicing the social skill of

(*continued*)

encouraging others to participate. Steven will be observed to determine his success at *staying with the group.* Students will be evaluated on their group paper (40%), their individual sections of the paper (30%), the unit test (20%), and group members' ratings of their group performance (10%). They will also engage in individual self-evaluation, as well as group reflection and goal setting, using forms provided by the teacher.

THE ADVANTAGES OF COOPERATIVE LEARNING

Johnson and Johnson (1989) document more than 800 studies that have been conducted on cooperative learning. Meta-analyses and reviews of these studies indicate that cooperative learning situations, as opposed to individualistic and competitive learning situations, result in higher student achievement, increased student self-esteem, and improved peer relations (Johnson & Johnson, 1989; Johnson, Johnson, & Maruyama, 1983; Johnson, Maruyama, Johnson, Nelson, & Skon, 1981, Slavin, 1990). When an educator considers employing an instructional approach, one of the first questions he or she will want addressed is: will this method enhance student learning? Based on a century of research on cooperative learning, it appears that this method enhances student learning under certain conditions. Although it is not possible to discuss this research fully in this chapter, aspects of the literature are highlighted below.

Academic Achievement

Slavin (1990) used a form of best-evidence synthesis to review 60 studies that examined the achievement effects of cooperative learning when used with small groups of elementary or secondary students. To be included in this review, the studies had to meet the following criteria: 1) cooperative learning groups had to be compared with control groups studying the same material; 2) the initial experimental and control groups had to be equivalent in order to control for pretest differences; 3) the duration of the study had to be at least 4 weeks (20 classroom hours); and 4) the achievement measures had to assess whether the objectives had been attained in the experimental and control classes, or a standardized test had to have been used. Effect size—the proportion of a standard deviation by which one group exceeds another—was used to measure the impact of cooperative learning. An effect size of at least +.25 was considered to be significant. With respect to achievement outcomes, 49 of the 68 comparisons were positive (72%), favoring cooperative learning methods, while only 8 (12%) favored control groups. The investigation found variations in achievement effects among the different types of cooperative learning methods. It was found that positive achievement outcomes are most likely to occur when the conditions of positive interdependence and individual accountability are ensured.

Improved Self-Esteem

Another important outcome of cooperative learning is the positive effects on student self-esteem that can result from this method. Self-esteem is defined as a judgement about one's own worth; it is based on how well-liked and competent a person feels. Improved self-esteem can result from achieving challenging goals, from gaining the respect of others, and from favorable comparisons with others. Using a meta-analysis methodology, Johnson and Johnson (1989) reviewed the research on cooperative, individualistic, and competitive learning as they relate to self-esteem. A meta-analysis combines the results of independent studies that test the same hypotheses. By quantifying the findings of studies using a common metric, inferential statistics are used to draw conclusions about the overall result of the studies (Glass, McGraw, & Smith, 1981). The Johnsons' meta-analysis identified 77 studies on self-esteem and social interdependence. About 53% of the findings were statistically significant in favor of cooperation, while less than 1% favored competition. The average cooperator's self-esteem was 3/5 of a standard deviation higher than the average competitor's self-esteem and 2/5 of a standard deviation higher than that of the average person working independently. The data also indicate that working individualistically is generally better for one's self-esteem than working competitively (effect size = 0.19). The z-score indicates that the likelihood of these findings being due to chance is less than 1 in 3,000 (it would take over 3,000 studies to reduce the z-score to nonsignificance). This meta-analysis shows that cooperative learning can help children to value themselves and to perceive themselves positively.

In addition to higher achievement and increased self-esteem, cooperative learning also produces more active learners, provides opportunities for improving social skills, and fosters greater peer acceptance.

Active Learning

Students working in cooperative groups are encouraged to discuss and apply what they are learning. In cooperative activities, the students themselves often become teachers within the groups. Most experienced teachers would agree that it is when you teach that you learn the most: as Seneca, the Roman philosopher said, "Qui docet discit"—whoever teaches learns twice. Students participating in cooperative learning groups also hear more explanations and are exposed to a greater variety of strategies for solving problems (Johnson & Johnson, 1989).

In cooperative situations, students talk about problems, a form of cognitive rehearsal and elaboration that assists in understanding and retaining material. Sometimes peer explanations are more helpful to students than adult explanations because they are given by someone at a similar cognitive-developmental level. Student "translations" of material may be quite novel and sometimes very effective. Ten-year-old Aaron, who was making a presentation on carnivorous plants to a 1st-grade class, gave his own example of what "carnivorous" meant. He asked the children if they knew who Tyrannosaurus Rex was. Of course, the students knew T. Rex, the flesh-eating dinosaur. He then went on to show how some exotic plants (Venus Fly Traps, Sundews, and Pitcher Plants) were carnivorous like T. Rex because they consumed the "flesh" of insects, although a bit more passively, by trapping the insect in a sticky substance and then slowly digesting it. Ten-year-old Amy Turnbull (Turnbull & Bronicki, 1988), whose brother is disabled, made a presentation about mental retardation to a 2nd-grade class. She showed a film to the class about the Special Olympics and read to them from a book.

> I told them that people who are mentally retarded learn slower than us. But they can still learn. I also said that brains are like a record player, because they work on different speeds. They learned that music is played on both slow and fast speeds. I told them that brains of kids with mental retardation work slowly and our brains work fast, but all of us can learn and have happy lives. (p. 34)

Social Skill Development

It is through interpersonal interaction that individuals observe, perform, and receive feedback on social behaviors, which makes cooperative learning activities especially beneficial for students with learning and behavior problems. Carefully structured cooperative activities provide an opportunity for teachers to observe student behavior and make decisions about which social/cooperative skills merit greater attention. Then, teachers systematically instruct students in these specific areas, monitoring performance and providing feedback. Cooperative learning activities are an excellent context in which to develop leadership skills, conflict resolution skills, and interpersonal communication skills.

Putnam, Rynders, Johnson, and Johnson (1989) studied the effects of social skill instruction on the behavior of students with moderate and severe disabilities and those of their peers without disabilities in cooperative learning groups in 5th-grade science classes. The cooperative learning method entailed adapting the instructional methods and objectives for the unit on displacement to allow participation by students with disabilities. Students who received the cooperative skill instruction interacted more frequently by "orienting" and making "positive comments" to one another than those who did not.

Investigations of the effects of cooperative learning activities (teams–games–tournament) on the social behavior of adolescents with emotional disturbance was observed by Slavin (1977). Similarly, Janke (1978) recorded improvements in on-task time and a drop in disruptive behavior for students engaged in cooperative learning. Achievement gains were nonsignificant in both studies, but more-frequent peer interactions, a primary goal for these students, were observed in a generalization setting in a follow-up study.

In addition to practicing social skills during cooperative activities, some students may need systematic training and direct instruction in this area. Such programs exist; Goldstein, Sprafkin, Gershaw, and Klein's (1983) structured learning approach for teaching social competencies is one example of this strategy. Structured learning employs a group format for directly teaching social skills. Using modeling, role playing, and performance feedback, one skill at a time is taught and then transferred to training in other settings. *Skillstreaming the Elementary School Child* (McGinnis, Goldstein, Sprafkin, & Gershaw, 1984) is an excellent resource for teachers of children with behavior disorders.

One of the best opportunities for students to learn and practice social skills is in cooperative group situations. If some students need extra support and reinforcement (e.g., preteaching, rewards) in order to acquire certain skills, then cooperative learning procedures can be combined with structured learning to maximize social skill acquisition.

Peer Acceptance and Friendship

Researchers have shown that cooperative learning experiences foster friendships among classmates. Peer acceptance has been measured by asking students to respond to questions about "who they like in the class"; or to rank their friends in the class; or to rate other students according to the degree to which they like to work or play with them, using a likert scale. Students with disabilities are also more accepted by other students in cooperative learning situations than in competitive or individualistic situations (Ballard, Corman, Gottlieb, & Kaufman, 1977; Johnson & Johnson, 1984, 1989; Johnson et al., 1983), even when these students are not effective contributors to the success of a group.

Deutsch (1949) once theorized that individuals who facilitate the achievement of one's goals are liked and accepted, and that individuals who frustrate one's goal attainment are disliked and rejected, a theory that has been referred to as the "bumbler hypothesis." While group members will attempt to make up for the ineffective actions or performance of a group member, they will resent the actions of the "bumbler" (Johnson & Johnson, 1989). Years ago, I vividly recall swimming the 100-meter medley relay with a team of three other swimmers. During the meet, I was asked to swim the butterfly—my worst stroke—for an absent team member. Despite my best effort, I swam considerably more slowly than my opponent, and our team fell behind in the competition. Thankfully, the freestyle swimmer made up for my lost time and led the team to victory. Just as Deutsch hypothesized, the team members celebrated the performance of the freestyle swimmer, while their silence toward me made their frustration at my feeble butterfly attempt apparent. I was devastated. Fortunately, research tells us that this is not likely to happen with a truly cooperative team. Studies show that low-achieving individuals are actually liked better in cooperative situations than in competitive situations (Johnson, Johnson, & Scott, 1978). How is it that lower performance by a cooperative group member does not result in dislike and rejection? Johnson and Johnson (1989) theorized the following:

1. In cooperative activities, low-performing students are perceived by their peers in multi-dimensional (as opposed to stereotypic) and dynamic (as opposed to static) ways. Low-performing students are recognized for their areas of strengths, which are revealed over the course of ongoing and appropriately structured interactions.
2. Students tend to value high effort despite low ability. Therefore, if the low performer is trying hard in the group, he or she will be liked for making a good effort.
3. Students in cooperative groups have expectations that all members will help to facilitate the group's attainment of the goal. These expectations are generalized to the low performing group member—even when that person doesn't actually contribute to success.
4. Students like to assist low-performing peers. There is a norm of helping others in our society, and helpers become personally committed to doing so. This personal commitment is hypothesized to result in greater liking for the low-performing peer.

The fact that even low performers are liked and valued in cooperative groups, despite their areas of weakness, is good news for educators who are looking for ways to promote peer acceptance as they structure inclusive classrooms. (For a more thorough discussion of the Johnsons' theoretical explanation, see *Cooperative and Competition: Theory and Research*, 1989, pp. 113–114.)

COOPERATIVE LEARNING AND DIVERSE POPULATIONS

Cooperative learning has a long history in American schools that begins in the 1800s, when it was emphasized during the Common School Movement. In the 1930s, John Dewey advocated for cooperative learning as part of his project method of instruction, but since then, individualistic and competitive learning structures have predominated in American schools. The passage of the Civil Rights Act of 1954 prompted educational researchers to re-examine the potential of cooperative learning for promoting the desegregation of formerly all-white schools. Numerous studies were conducted in order to determine whether cooperative learning promoted more positive cross-ethnic relationships. In their book *Cooperation and Competition: Theory and Research*, Johnson and Johnson (1989) discuss this literature, concluding that the results of relevant studies "point towards interaction within a cooperative context as being a major determinant of whether cross-ethnic contact produced positive attitudes and relationships" (p. 125). Cooperative learning has also been beneficial for students with disabilities and students of Native American and those of Native Alaskan heritage.

Students with Disabilities

Over the last 2 decades, educators have also searched for ways to facilitate the integration of students with disabilities into inclusive classrooms. More than 50 of the studies on cooperative learning focus specifically on students with disabilities. The reviews by Johnson and Johnson (1981, 1989) and Slavin (1990) indicate that cooperative learning (versus individualistic and competitive learning) increases the academic achievement and social acceptance of students with disabilities. Johnson and Johnson (1989) found that cooperative learning experiences produce greater interpersonal attraction between students with and without disabilities than do competitive (effect size = 0.70) or individualistic (effect size = 0.16) activities. Most of these investigations have been conducted with students labeled mildly disabled (e.g., those with learning disabilities, mental retardation, or sensory and physical impairments). Student achievement has been studied in a variety of subject areas, such as mathematics, reading, writing, language arts, geography, music, science, and social science (Cosden, Pearl, & Bryan, 1985; Hine, Goldman, & Cosden, 1990; Johnson & Johnson, 1984, 1985; Lew & Bryant, 1984; Nevin, Johnson, & Johnson, 1982; Slavin, Madden, & Leavey 1984).

Cooperative learning investigations involving students with moderate and severe disabilities have been conducted in elementary and secondary schools and in recreational settings, and have included activities as varied as science projects, art, cooking, music, academic and pre-academic tasks, and group recreation activities such as bowling (Eichinger, 1990; Jellison, Brooks, & Huck, 1984; Johnson, Johnson, De Weerdt, Lyons, & Zaidman, 1983; Johnson, Rynders, Johnson, Schmidt, & Haider, 1979; Putnam et al., 1989; Rynders, Johnson, Johnson, & Schmidt, 1980; Wilcox, Sbardellati, & Nevin, 1987; also see the annotated bibliography by Putnam and Farnsworth-Lunt, 1989, for article abstracts). The general findings of this research are positive: Cooperative learning is associated with significantly higher levels of certain positive social and verbal interaction behaviors, greater interpersonal attraction (according to sociometric outcome measures), and academic gains comparable to those achieved in competitive and individualistic situations.

Some researchers have criticized the methodologies employed in studies on the effects of cooperative learning for students with disabilities. One such concern is the preponderance of short-term experimental investigations lasting from 3 to 6 weeks (Slavin, 1990). Such brief investigations do not address the effects of cooperative learning situations on the more lasting relationships among students, which are likely to fluctuate over time. Lloyd, Crowley, Kohler, and Strain (1988) agreed that the research evidence on the effects of cooperative learning in reducing social rejection is substantial, but that questions remain about the method's effects on academic achievement. These researchers concluded that we have yet to demonstrate that cooperative learning works better than individualized instruction or other instructional interventions with well-established records of effectiveness.

Slavin, Leavey, and Madden (1984) compared cooperative learning to individualized instruction, finding them to be equally effective in increasing the math achievement levels of mainstreamed students with academic disabilities. They compared team-assisted individualization (TAI) with individualized instruction (II) and a traditional method of teaching mathematics. In this study, 117 students with mild academic disabilities were mainstreamed with 387 nondisabled students in 18 classes (grades 3–5). TAI is an instructional approach that combines cooperative learning and individualized instruction using teams and a team-study method. TAI was found to have particularly strong effects on the social acceptance of mainstreamed students, on the development of friendships, on students' attitudes toward math, and on teachers' ratings of behavior. No significant differences were found between groups on math achievement, although students performed better in the classes employing TAI and II than in the control classes.

Native American and Native Alaskan Students

Cooperative learning appears to be highly consistent with the culture and values of many Native American groups. Swisher (1990), reviewed the literature on the cooperative nature of Native American and Native Alaskan children and concluded that cooperative learning was highly compatible with the learning and interactional style of some Native American children. Traditionally, these children avoid individual competition, emphasize cooperation, and shun being "singled out" in front of an audience. This is not to say that Indian children shun competition in general, but they dislike the type of competition that is often used in classrooms, that is, *individual* competition. These students do not wish to stand out in a group, a preference which has cultural roots and is still sanctioned today through teasing and other forms of peer pressure. Competition, however, has its place outside the classroom in the form of team sports (Brewer, 1977).

We have much to learn from cultural groups who historically have lived in accordance with cooperative values. Peter John, 93-year-old Chief of the Athabascan Indians of Alaska, recalls the traditional way of life:

> People used to go out and hunt together, have lunch together. They'd tell stories about what happened years ago. How to take care of themselves. How to stand up to danger. Don't listen to too much gossip.

For the Athabascan Indians, sharing is a way of life:

> Give whatever you got and you'll get in return something better than what you give. You believe that? You got to share. That's the old Indian way.
> (Hulen, 1993, p. 1-6)

MAJOR APPROACHES TO COOPERATIVE LEARNING

The field of cooperative learning is rich with approaches and strategies to match the needs of particular situations and students. While an in-depth discussion of all of the various approaches is not possible, those most widely used and researched are summarized in this section. What they all have in common is the incorporation of heterogeneous groups of students working toward a common goal.

The Conceptual Approach

David and Roger Johnson, who established the Cooperative Learning Center at the University of Minnesota, have spent the last 30 years researching cooperative learning and developing books and training materials for educators who work in a wide variety of settings, ranging from preschool through higher education. The Johnsons' method of cooperative learning has been referred to as the conceptual approach, because it is based on the assumption that teachers can learn the key principles of structuring effective cooperative learning activities (which are described in the first section of this chapter) and then tailor them to suit the needs of their own students. The teacher becomes the "academic expert" and "classroom manager" and should be able to experiment with the procedures over time. Cooperative teams of teachers are beneficial in supporting the application of cooperative learning procedures in classrooms and among colleagues in schools and communities.

There are a number of distinguishing features of the Johnsons' approach to cooperative learning. First, they place great emphasis on cooperative-skill development. The Johnsons believe that cooperative skills should be taught directly to students, as discussed above in the section on social-skill development. They also stress the critical importance of positive interdependence and elaborate on numerous ways in which teachers can structure activities that encourage positive interdependence, as well as other types of interdependence such as fantasy interdependence, identity interdependence, and outside-enemy interdependence, to name just a few.

The Johnsons have not developed specific curricula; rather, they stress the cooperative learning process and generic cooperative structures that can be used in any content area. Group structures range from relatively formal structures, such as a "jigsaw" or a "cooperative peer editing" structure, to informal activities such as "simultaneous explanation pairs" or "closure focussed discussion pairs" (see *Cooperative Learning Lesson Structures* by Johnson & Johnson, 1991). The Johnsons have developed generic lesson-plan formats, as well as several books containing lesson plans suitable for all levels.

The conceptual approach has been applied at all levels of the educational system and is increasingly an influence on teams of educators, students, parents, specialists, and community members who are making decisions and solving problems. Numerous articles and books on strategies for dapting curricula and designing materials for cooperative learning are available from the Cooperative Learning Center at the University of Minnesota.

The Curricular Approach

Robert Slavin and his associates at Johns Hopkins University have developed curriculum-specific cooperative approaches to support instruction in heterogeneous classrooms. Two of their models, team accelerated instruction (TAI) and cooperative integrated reading and composition (CIRC), are alternatives to pull-out programs and the ability grouping of low-achieving students.

TAI (Slavin, Leavey, & Madden, 1984) combines individualized instruction with team work in mathematics. The curriculum covers addition, subtraction, multiplication, division, numeration, decimals, fractions, word problems, statistics, and algebra. Students work together in heterogeneous teams to help one another, to check one another's quizzes and homework, and to review team scores. Students work on self-instructional materials at the appropriate ability level. They also receive group instruction, along with other students who are working on the same curriculum level, from the teacher. If a student fails to achieve an 80% success criterion for the unit, the teacher intervenes to provide the necessary individualized instruction.

CIRC is a program for teaching reading and writing in the upper elementary grades (Slavin, 1990; Stevens, Slavin, & Madden, 1991). Using basal reading books and reading groups much like those used in traditional reading programs, students follow a sequence of teacher instruction, team practice, team pre-assessments, and quizzes. Some features of this program are team rewards, equal opportunity for success, and individual accountability. Team rewards consist of certificates issued to teams based on the average performance of all team members on all reading and writing activities. Students have equal opportunities for success because they work on materials appropriate to their own reading levels. Individual accountability is ensured because students take individual quizzes and write individual compositions that contribute to team scores.

The CIRC program was tested with students with academic disabilities in remedial reading pull-out programs and those receiving "pull-in" regular classroom instruction. It was found that the greater the integration of students with academic disabilities, the greater the achievement benefits to them. Special education students in CIRC gained the equivalent of ½–⅔ of a grade more than their peers in traditional pull-out programs (Stevens et al., 1991). "CIRC gives teachers strategies to accommodate the students' needs without detracting from the education of the rest of the students. The student interaction in cooperative groups also furthers the goals of mainstreaming by increasing the social acceptance of special education students" (Stevens et al., 1991, p. 18).

In addition to these cooperative learning programs that are specific to certain curricular areas, the Johns Hopkins researchers have developed and researched two general cooperative learning methods that can be adapted to most subject areas and grade levels: student teams–achievement divisions (STAD) and teams–games–tournament (TGT). In STAD, the students work together in heterogeneous teams of four to master the assigned material and then take individual quizzes. Students' quiz scores are then compared to their past averages, and each student earns improvement points if he or she has exceeded his or her former average. Individual students' improvement scores are totaled to calculate team scores. If the teams meet certain criteria, they receive some type of reward (e.g., a certificate). This cycle of activities takes about 3–5 class periods. Students are encouraged to help others in their group to learn the material. All students can contribute to the teams success by improving their past scores, thus, low performers can contribute as much or more than high performers (Slavin, 1990).

Teams–games–tournament is much like STAD, but replaces the quizzes with weekly tournaments that involve individual competition between members of opposing teams (Slavin, 1990). The teams are heterogeneous, and students compete against peers with similar records of performance.

Curriculum units, books, and video tapes can be ordered from the Team Learning Project, Johns Hopkins University.

The Structural Approach

The work of Spencer Kagan (1990) has developed into what is known as the structural approach to cooperative learning. A structure is a content-independent way of organizing social interaction in the classroom. Kagan bases his method of cooperative learning on a research and theory tradition purporting that our behaviors are determined, to a large extent, by the particular situations in which we are placed. Kagan feels that people often underestimate the extreme importance of situational variables, which can lead to either cooperative or competitive approaches to accomplishing a goal.

A *structure* consists of a series of specific steps and prescribed behaviors that can be used with a variety of academic content. A number of different structures have been formulated, each having different functions, which Kagan refers to as "domains of usefulness." Different structures are appropriate in classrooms to achieve the following outcomes: 1) promoting mastery of material, 2) fostering concept development, 3) team building, 4) classbuilding, 5) communication building, and 6) multifunctional uses. Numbered Heads Together is an example of a typical structure:

Numbered Heads Together
1.   Students form teams and count off so each student has a number.
2.   A question is posed to the students.
3.   The students are asked to "put their heads together" to assure that everyone knows the answer.
4.   The teacher calls out a number and the students with that number raise their hands or stand up to respond. (Kagan, 1990, p. 13)

This structure guarantees positive interdependence because students "put their heads together" to agree on the correct answer and to ensure that all team members know that answer. Individual accountability is established by randomly calling a student number, thus, everyone anticipates being called on. Numbered Heads Together is useful for review situations that emphasize knowledge and comprehension of information.

A variety of structures have been developed for classroom use, and advice is provided on when to use each particular structure and on how to use structures in combination with other instructional strategies. Kagan (1990) suggested the use of "a structure a month" in staff-development activities. Collegial support groups can coach one another and provide support in adapting structures to specific classroom needs.

Complex Instructional Approach

Elizabeth Cohen, Director of the Stanford Program for Complex Instruction at Stanford University, has developed a model of cooperative learning for use in heterogeneous classrooms. According to Cohen (1991b, p. 4), "Too many students do not have the resources to profit from traditional instruction with grade-level materials." She believes that it is time to stop focusing on "high," "medium," and "low" intellectual abilities and, instead, to consider different *kinds* of intellectual abilities. Cohen's perspective is consistent with Gardner's work on the theory of multiple intelligences, which expands on the idea that intelligence is multidimensional (Gardner, 1983). In *Frames of Mind*, Gardner identified seven intelligences: linguistic, musical, logical–mathematical, spatial, bodily–kinesthetic, interpersonal intelligence, and intrapersonal intelligence. Cohen and her colleagues have developed a program that is designed to facilitate the development of thinking skills and to enhance the linguistic and academic functioning of children in heterogeneous classrooms.

The complex instructional approach is designed for use with elementary students in grades two through five. Students are involved in activities that are challenging and intrinsically motivating. Complex tasks that require multiple abilities are assigned. In addition to incorporating the traditional academic skills (reading, writing, and arithmetic), lessons may require artistic abilities, reasoning abilities, observation skills, social skills, skills in discerning spatial relationships, and many others. Students work in groups, using one another as resources to complete the assignment. Group roles such as Materials Manager, Harmonizer, and Resource Person, are assigned to individual students. Curricular materials are designed to include activities that are open ended and require higher-order thinking. The use of typical drill and textbook or workbook materials is discouraged. Finding Out/Descubrimiento is a bilingual math and science curriculum based on complex instruction (Cohen, 1991a, p. 4). This curriculum is designed around themes such as crystals and powders, balance and structures, clocks and pendulums, reflection/refraction and optical illusions. The intention is to select themes that are highly motivating to students. Materials include activity cards, manipulatives, and worksheets (Lotan & Benton, 1990).

To raise expectations for low-status students, teachers discuss the various abilities that are required in the group work, emphasizing that all the skills and abilities are important and relevant to the task. Teachers specifically point out the competence of low-status students by commenting publicly on what these children are doing well and how important their contributions are to the group. Candida Graves (Graves & Graves, 1991) recounts an experience in her classroom with a student named Juan who had a poor academic record and rarely spoke in class (his first language was Spanish and he had only been in the U.S. for a few years). The other students generally paid very little attention to Juan. One day Graves was observing a cooperative group of students working on a decimal activity and noticed that Juan was the only one in his group who had the right answer. She said "Juan! You have figured out this worksheet correctly. You understand how decimals work. You really understand that kind of notation. Can you explain it to your group?" (p. 14). After circulating around the room, she returned to find Juan explaining what he understood to the other students. Other students in the class began to call him 'the smart one' and eventually this nickname spread to his neighborhood. Pointing out successes is an excellent way to increase a child's self-esteem and motivation to learn.

TEACHING IN INCLUSIVE CLASSROOMS REQUIRES A REPERTOIRE OF INSTRUCTIONAL APPROACHES

A barrier to the success of students with learning or behavior problems in regular classes has been that, in the past, teachers and school personnel felt compelled to teach all students with the same approaches—usually teacher-dominated, whole-class instruction (Goodlad, 1983). Often, teachers simply resort to teaching in the same way that they have been taught by unimaginative professors in university or college teacher-education programs. Sometimes, teachers find it logistically difficult to use a variety of approaches, or they may not have been exposed to a variety of methodologies in their own education or through inservice training.

In all likelihood, students with diverse educational needs will require some degree of individualized tutoring in addition to cooperative learning activities. For example, many students have overcome difficulties in learning to read by receiving individualized instruction in comprehensive, holistic programs such as Reading Recovery (Clay, 1987), in which 1/2-hour tutorials are conducted three times a week. The lessons consist of reading small books and composing brief stories or messages, and a strategies approach is used to teach analytic skills. Teachers are trained to keep running records of each child's reading behavior and to use the results to analyze the types of cues that the child is employing. By examining the strategies, or mental operations, that the child is employing to derive meaning from text and the errors that he or she is making, the teachers determine how to best teach a comprehensive and balanced set of reading strategies for that particular child (Lyons, 1989). Data indicate that Reading Recovery has enabled many students with reading difficulties to return to the regular reading program after 30 or fewer sessions. If a student needs extra help with reading, then it should be provided by a qualified reading teacher or teacher's assistant. A tutorial can be conducted within the classroom or in a quiet space in the school at specified times during the day. Individualized tutoring for reading does not preclude participating in cooperative learning activities or other types of instruction. Indeed, cooperative learning groups for whole-language activities should reinforce what is learned in the tutorials.

It must be emphasized that the success of cooperative learning is in large part determined by the *quality* of the activity that students are asked to participate in. If cooperative learning is simply used for completing repetitious drill and practice worksheets as part of a lock-step, skills-based curriculum, it is unlikely that students will be motivated to do their best work or to exercise creativity or employ higher-order reasoning abilities. It is even more unlikely that such a curriculum will promote the success of a diversity of learners with various abilities, backgrounds, and learning styles. Authentic cooperative learning activities (Glasser, 1986) encourage students to demonstrate learning outcomes that have relevance and enable a child to succeed in his or her current and future environments. The greater the input of students themselves in the selection of topics and themes for cooperative learning, the more motivated and empowered they will be to become self-directed learners.

The learning styles of individual students must be taken into account when a determination is made regarding which instructional approach is the most effective. If one method doesn't work, then try another way! Cooperative learning is only one way to teach, but it is an approach that has been underutilized by educators, and those who do use it sometimes lack the theoretical understandings that lead to generalized applications at various levels of the school organization.

CONCLUDING COMMENTS

Educators facing the challenge of teaching a diversity of students in their classrooms are discovering that a cooperative approach to adult problem-solving and student learning has tremendous potential. When cooperative learning is coupled with effective instructional approaches and sound curricular adaptations for students with diverse learning styles and needs, benefits accrue to all students. Cooperative teaming enables educators, parents, specialists, teaching assistants, and others to practice skills in planning and problemsolving, often generating creative and innovative solutions.

Cooperative group learning is not a panacea for solving all of the problems that arise when teaching heterogeneous groups of students. However, it is one of many instructional methods that a teacher should have in his or her repertoire. Cooperative learning is critically important because it provides a context in which students can interact positively and a systematic method of instruction that emphasizes positive interdependence, individual accountability, active learning, and the acquisition of social skills. Furthermore, cooperative learning is an instructional tool that capitalizes on one of the greatest untapped educational resources available—the students themselves (Slavin, 1987). In the chapters that follow, practical suggestions are provided for using cooperative learning and other approaches and strategies to effectively meet students' needs in heterogeneous classrooms.

REFERENCES

Ballard, M., Corman, L., Gottlieb, J., & Kaufman, M.J. (1977). Improving the social status of mainstreamed retarded children. *Journal of Educational Psychology, 69*, 605–611.

Brewer, A. (1977). On Indian education. *Integrateducation, 15*, 21–23.

Clay, M. (1987). Implementing reading recovery: Systemic adaptations to an educational innovation. *New Zealand Journal of Educational Studies, 22*(1), 35–57.

Cohen, E.G. (1991a). Finding out/descubrimiento: Complex instruction in science. *Cooperative Learning, 1*, 30–31.

Cohen, E. (1991b). Strategies for creating a multi-ability classroom. *Cooperative Learning, 12*(1), 4–8.

Cosden, M., Pearl, R., & Bryan, T. (1985). The effects of cooperative and individual goal structures on learning disabled and non–learning disabled students. *Exceptional Children, 52*, 103–114.

Deutsch, M. (1949). A theory of cooperation and competition. *Human Relations, 2*, 199–231.

Eichinger, J. (1990). Effects of goal structures on social interaction between elementary level nondisabled students and students with severe disabilities. *Exceptional Children, 56*, 408–417.

Gardner, H. (1983). *Frames of mind.* New York: Basic Books.

Glass, G., McGraw, B., & Smith, M. (1981). *Meta-analysis in social research,* Beverly Hills: Sage Publications.

Glasser, W. (1986). *Control theory in the classroom.* New York: Harper and Row.

Goldstein, A.P., Sprafkin, R.P., Gershaw, N.J., & Klein, P. (1983). Structured learning: A psychoeducational approach for teaching social competencies. *Behavior Disorders, 8*(3), 161–170.

Goodlad, J.I. (1983). A study of schooling: Some findings and hypotheses. *Phi Delta Kappan, 64*, 462–470.

Graves, N., & Graves, T. (1991) Candida Graves: Complex teamwork in action. *Cooperative Learning, 12*(1), 12–16.

Hine, M.S., Goldman, S.R., & Cosden, M.A. (1990). Error monitoring by learning handicapped students engaged in collaborative microcomputer-based writing. *The Journal of Special Education, 23*(4), 407–422.

Hulen, D. (1993). The words he lives by. *Anchorage Daily News,* February 14, 1993, 1–7.

Janke, R. (1978, April). *The teams-games-tournament (TGT) method and the behavioral adjustment and academic achievement of emotionally impaired adolescents.* Paper presented at the annual meeting of the American Educational Research Association, Toronto.

Jellison, J.A., Brooks, B.H., & Huck, A.M. (1984). Structuring small groups and music reinforcement to facilitate positive interactions and acceptance of severely handicapped students in the regular music classroom. *Journal of Research in Music Education, 32*, 243–264.

Johnson, D.W., & Johnson, R. (1984). Building acceptance of differences between handicapped and nonhandicapped students: The effects of cooperative and individualistic instruction. *The Journal of Social Psychology, 122*, 257–267.

Johnson, D.W., & Johnson, R. (1985). Mainstreaming hearing-impaired students: The effect of effort in communicating on cooperation and interpersonal attraction. *Journal of Psychology, 119*, 31–44.

Johnson, D.W., & Johnson, R.T. (1989). *Cooperation and competition: Theory and Research.* Edina, MN: Interaction Books.

Johnson, D.W., & Johnson, R.T. (1991). *Cooperative learning lesson structures.* Edina, MN: Interaction Book Company.

Johnson, D.W., Johnson, D.W., DeWeerdt, N., Lyons, V., & Zaidman, B. (1983). Integrating severely handicapped seventh-grade students into constructive relationships with nonhandicapped peers in science class. *American Journal of Mental Deficiency, 87*, 611–619.

Johnson, D.W., Johnson, R.T., & Holubec, E.J. (1990). *Cooperation in the classroom* (rev. ed.). Edina, MN: Interaction Books.

Johnson, D.W., Johnson, R.T., & Maruyama, G. (1983). Interdependence and interpersonal attraction among heterogeneous and homogeneous individuals: A theoretical formulation and a meta-analysis of the research. *Review of Educational Research, 53*, 5–54.

Johnson, D.W., Johnson, R.T., & Scott, L. (1978). The effects of cooperative and individualized instruction on student attitudes and achievement. *The Journal of Social Psychology, 104*, 207–216.

Johnson, D., Maruyama, G., Johnson, R., Nelson, D., & Skon, L. (1981). The effects of cooperative, competitive, and individualistic goal structures on achievement: A meta-analysis. *Psychological Bulletin, 89*, 47–62.

Johnson, R.T., & Johnson, D.W. (1981). Building friendships between handicapped and non-handicapped students: Effects of cooperative and individualistic instruction. *American Educational Research Journal, 18*(4), 415–423.

Johnson, R., Rynders, J., Johnson, D.W., Schmidt, B., & Haider, S. (1979). Interaction between handicapped and nonhandicapped teenagers as a function of situational goal structuring: Implications for mainstreaming. *American Educational Research Journal, 16*, 161–167.

Joyce, B. (1992). Cooperative learning and staff development. *Cooperative Learning, 12*(2), 10–13.

Kagan, S. (1990). A structural approach to cooperative learning. *Educational Leadership, 47*(4), 12–15.

Lew, M., & Bryant, R. (1984). The effects of cooperative groups on regular class spelling achievement of special needs learners. *Educational Psychology, 4*, 275–283.

Lloyd, J.W., Crowley, E.W., Kohler, F.W., & Strain, P.S. (1988). Redefining the applied research agenda: Cooperative learning, prereferral, teacher consultation, and peer-mediated interventions. *Journal of Learning Disabilities, 21*, 43–52.

Lotan, R., & Benton, J. (1990). Finding out about complex instruction: Teaching math and science in heterogeneous classrooms. In N. Davidson (Ed.), *Cooperative learning in mathematics: A handbook for teachers* (pp. 47–68). Reading, MA: Addison Wesley.

Lyons, C.A. (1989). Reading recovery: An effective early intervention program that can prevent mislabeling children as learning disabled. *ERS Spectrum, 7*(4), 3–8.

McGinnis, E., Goldstein, A.P., Sprafkin, R.P., & Gershaw, N.J. (1984). *Skill-streaming the elementary school child: A guide for teaching prosocial skills.* Champaign, IL: Research Press Company.

Nevin, A., Johnson, D.W., & Johnson, R. (1982). Effects of group and individual contingencies on academic performance and social relations of special needs students. *Journal of Social Psychology, 116,* 41–59.

Putnam, J.W., & Farnsworth-Lunt, J. (1989). *Cooperative learning and the integration of students with disabilities: An annotated bibliography.* Missoula, MT: The Montana University Affiliated Program, Institute for Human Resources.

Putnam, J.W., Rynders, J.E., Johnson, R., & Johnson, D. (1989). Collaborative skill instruction for promoting positive interactions between mentally handicapped and nonhandicapped children. *Exceptional Children, 55,* 550–558.

Rynders, J., Johnson, R., Johnson, D.W., & Schmidt, B. (1980). Producing positive interaction among Down's Syndrome and nonhandicapped teenagers through cooperative goal structuring. *American Journal of Mental Deficiency, 85,* 268–273.

Slavin, R.E. (1977). A student team approach to teaching adolescents with special emotional and behavioral needs. *Psychology in the Schools, 14*(1), 77–84.

Slavin, R.E. (1987). Cooperative learning and the cooperative school. *Educational Leadership, 45*(3), 7–13.

Slavin, R.E. (1990). *Cooperative learning: Theory, research and practice.* Englewood Cliffs, NJ: Prentice Hall.

Slavin, R.E., Leavey, M.B., & Madden, N.A. (1984). Combining cooperative learning and individualized instruction: Effects on student mathematics achievement, attitudes, and behaviors. *Elementary School Journal, 84,* 409–422.

Slavin, R.E., Madden, N.A., & Leavey, M. (1984). Effects of team assisted individualization on the mathematics achievement of academically handicapped students and nonhandicapped students. *Journal of Educational Psychology, 76,* 813–819.

Stevens, R., Slavin, R., & Madden, N. (1991). Cooperative integrated reading and composition (CIRC): Effective cooperative learning in reading and language arts. *Cooperative Learning, 11*(4), 16–18.

Swisher, K. (1990). Cooperative learning and the education of American Indian/ Alaskan Native Students: A review of the literature and suggestions for implementation. *Journal of American Indian Education, 29*(2), 36–43.

Turnbull, A., & Bronicki, J.B. (1988). Changing second graders' attitudes toward people with mental retardation: Using kid power. *Mental Retardation, 24*(1), 44–45.

Wilcox, J., Sbardellati, E., & Nevin, A. (1987). Cooperative learning groups aid integration. *Teaching Exceptional Children, 20*(1), 61–63.

3

Curricular and Instructional Adaptations for Including Students with Disabilities in Cooperative Groups

ANN NEVIN

In order for students to be success-
ful in the rapidly approaching twenty-first century, they will need to
know how to live and work with people who are *different*: different col-
ors, different ethnicities, different cultures, and different abilities. Benjamin (1989) urges that school curricula not only teach students how to
communicate but also provide practice in collaborating with other people who may hold different opinions. Cooperative learning has this capacity: cooperative learning groups can help any student achieve his or
her own academic goals while assisting others at the same time.

Success in employing cooperative learning is ensured if cooperative
lessons are carefully planned and if the collaborative skills that students
are to learn are consciously practiced by the adults who are teaching them.
Johnson, Johnson, and Holubec (1987) delineate an 8-step method for
planning cooperative lessons:

1. Select an academic instructional objective and materials correlated
   to IEP objectives for students with disabilities.
2. Select the group size and assign the students to groups in such a way
   as to ensure heterogeneity and diversity within each group.
3. Arrange the classroom in clusters to ensure face-to-face interaction
   among students and ease of mobility between groups.

4. Design the cooperative goal structure to incorporate goal, reward, and resource interdependence.
5. Specify the criteria for student success in both the academic tasks and in cooperative interactions.
6. Monitor group and individual performance through direct observation.
7. Intervene when necessary to teach academic or cooperative skills.
8. Evaluate both academic task achievement and cooperative skills performance.

These steps follow a traditional lesson-plan format, with the addition of three critical elements: 1) positive interdependence (with individual accountability), 2) structured practice in collaborative skills, and 3) scheduling of time to evaluate the relation between cooperative skills and achievement. This chapter outlines curricular and instructional adaptations of these eight steps designed to ensure the success of cooperative learning in inclusive classrooms. But before elaborating on these steps, let us first examine some basic issues related to making curricular decisions.

MAKING CURRICULAR DECISIONS

The first step in the teacher's role in cooperative learning—selecting the appropriate instructional objective and materials—sounds simple, but it is actually quite complex, because it often requires cooperation among teachers, parents, specialists, and others who are involved in the life of a student with different educational needs. Teachers who have adopted cooperative learning in order to include students with disabilities in the general education classroom know that they must make many critical curricular decisions to accommodate these students' various needs. One important decision is whether the student will be required to learn all of the general education content in a curriculum area, a subset of that content, or completely different content (perhaps that from a lower grade level). Every educator should go far beyond simply knowing what a student's IEP objectives are (although being informed about the IEP objectives *is* a teacher's basic right and responsibility); successful heterogeneous cooperative learning requires: 1) a basic understanding of the principles of recommended educational practices related to curriculum, 2) expansion of curriculum objectives to accommodate diversity, 3) adaptation of the curriculum, and 4) evaluation of achievement.

Principles of Recommended Educational Practices

Recommended practices are those that have been identified by researchers and practitioners as being most likely to further students' achievements in desired directions. Some elements of recommended practices for students with especially challenging educational needs that most directly affect curriculum are:

Providing chronological age–appropriate curriculum objectives and materials Teachers should make sure that no matter what a student's performance level, the objectives and materials are appropriately similar to those provided for her or his chronological-age peers. For example, a 15-year-old functioning at the level of a 6-year-old should not be given 1st-grade worksheets and crayons for a math assignment, but instead should receive computer-assisted instruction.

Structuring social integration Teachers should consciously schedule direct, meaningful, and consistent interaction between students with and those without disabilities. Cooperative learning lessons are beneficial because they require that students work together socially to achieve academic objectives.

Designing functional curricula Teachers should rewrite standard curricular objectives in accordance with the likely demands of future environments in which students will be expected to function independently. As an example, the 15-year-old student who performs at a 6-year-old level in math might be assigned curriculum objectives that focus on practicing basic math by having the student keep score for a school recreational activity.

Integrating services Teachers should collaborate with related service providers (e.g., speech therapists, physical therapists) to coordinate curriculum objectives in all areas. They should arrange for the unobtrusive delivery of necessary services with the least possible amount of disruption or segregation from the routines of typical students.

It should be noted that there are many other recommended practices for ensuring the appropriate education of students with disabilities (such as family participation in developing the individual educational program, and nondiscriminatory assessment) that may have implications for adapting cooperative learning lessons. In addition, recommended practices are continuously developed and refined. Thus, teachers need to bring an open mind to the design process for cooperative learning lessons.

Expanding the Classroom Curriculum To Accommodate Diversity

Task analyses and *overlapping curriculum objectives* are two elements that teachers can use to expand the possible curriculum options for students in their classrooms. Task analyses involve sequencing some of the curriculum in carefully detailed, step-by-step portions so that many students can work independently. Some students, of course, may do better if they work with a partner or an instructional aide to receive the modeling or coaching that they need. Researchers have already designed a number of curriculum sequences in the areas of math, phonics, vocabulary, and comprehension or thinking skills. (See Idol, Nevin, & Paolucci-Whitcomb, 1986, for detailed descriptions of how to task analyze various standard curricula in reading, mathematics, and dictionary skills.)

A disadvantage of task-analyzed curricula, however, is that students must often complete one set of tasks before being introduced to those that follow. Overlapping curriculum objectives (Giangreco & Putnam, 1991) enable each student to work at different levels in different subjects. For example, a student might be able to perform at the preschool level in reading, the 4th-grade level in creative writing, the 2nd-grade level in spelling, and the 5th-grade level in social studies or science; but physical disabilities might interfere with this student's demonstrating these capabilities. Giangreco, Cloninger, and Iverson (1990) give an example of curriculum overlapping for a group of students who are involved in the same cooperative lesson, but pursuing goals and objectives in different curricular areas: if a group of students is conducting a science lab to learn about electricity, a student with special needs might participate in order to pursue goals in the areas of communication and socialization, such as following directions, staying with the group, and pointing to the correct lab equipment.

Adapting Curriculum Objectives

A curriculum can be adapted in yet other ways for cooperative learning groups: student response modes can be changed, functional equivalents can be created, different completion rates can be assigned, varying workloads can be required, and computer-assisted instruction can be utilized.

Changing Response Modes   A response mode is the way in which a student is required to demonstrate his or her learning. Response modes are correlated with sensory abilities. Teachers ask students to write, speak, look, point, and/or listen; sometimes they encourage students to draw, paint, create objects (e.g., dioramas or story boxes), sing, dance, or demonstrate. Complex projects may require that a student use multiple response modes. Teachers should present a range of possible response modes. As an example of a way to adapt response modes, Putnam (1990) suggests that a "student could work on mobility skills by obtaining materials and handing in the finished product, or on communication skills by summarizing the story using sign language" (p. 12).

Developing Functional Equivalents   Teachers develop functional equivalents when they translate a curriculum objective. For example, an objective such as "complete 100 simple addition problems with 80% accuracy on a 3-minute timed test" may be translated into "can determine whether he or she has received the correct change when purchasing items." As an example, Putnam (1990) recommends the use of personalized objectives, whereby unique functional or interpersonal skills can be learned in the context of other curricular objectives.

Allowing for Different Completion Rates   Students often demonstrate individual differences in the amount of work that they are able to complete in a given time. Teachers can adjust the amount of work, as well as the time frame in which the work is to be completed.

Allowing for Different Workloads   Teachers can individualize requirements for students. As suggested by Putnam (1990), "the goal is not changed but the student is required to contribute less" (p. 12). Instead of completing 20 spelling words, for example, the student might only be required to complete 10.

Computer-Assisted Instruction   Computers can provide students with alternative response modes, as well as increased competence in self-expression. Teachers who combine computer-assisted instruction with cooperative learning can expect their students to benefit both cognitively and socially (see, for example, Cosden, 1989). Characteristics to be considered in selecting software for cooperative learning include: adaptability of software (to allow teachers to add new content or change parameters); ease of use for both teachers and students; large, easy-to-read displays; manuals at the appropriate reading level; and feedback that includes correction as well as reinforcement. Fink (1990) suggests that teachers who use computer-assisted instruction and cooperative learning to include students with disabilities construct groups of socially compatible students, teach social skills as well as fulfilling IEP goals, and invest time in helping teams to work together.

Evaluating Achievement

Adjusting the means of evaluating students is another important aspect of making curricular decisions. Several choices are available to fit the individual needs of students in inclusive classrooms (see also Villa & Thousand, chap. 4, this volume).

Criterion-Referenced Systems   Teachers who individualize their curricula to include students with disabilities in cooperative learning groups must select achievement tests that are criterion-referenced, as norm-referenced tests will, by definition, automatically place students with disabilities in the failing ranges. Norm-referenced systems discriminate against every student with differences, whether cultural, educational, or disabling.

Accountability for Individual and Group Performance
Teachers who conduct cooperative learning lessons regularly schedule individual assessments of students to ensure individual accountability for

achievement. Different criteria can be assigned to each student to accommodate individual differences. Group performance on assignments is also measured.

Personalized Evaluation   Teachers can individualize their evaluation systems to compensate for the sensory or intellectual differences of their students. As suggested by Putnam (1990), "expectations may be set at a lower grade or developmental level. In writing, for example, while other group members concern themselves with correct punctuation, the student with a disability can copy vocabulary words and define them" (p. 12).

Equal Opportunity for Success   Slavin (1990) suggests that cooperative learning is uniquely capable of ensuring that each person in the cooperative learning group is accountable for learning the specified content. When students contribute to their team's success by improving on their own past performance (i.e., when teacher's grade students on improvement), then each student has an equal opportunity to be a successful team member.

MAKING INSTRUCTIONAL DECISIONS

The most important instructional decision, of course, is the initial decision to use cooperative groups. The following discussion elaborates on the instructional decisions correlated with the Johnsons' eight steps of the teacher's role.

Group Size and Membership

There are multiple methods and procedures for choosing the membership, size, duration, and purpose of cooperative learning groups. Over the course of a school year, students can be assured that they will be members of core groups, formal groups, and temporary groups.

Core Groups   The major purpose of core groups is to provide a sense of affiliation and bonding with other class members. Core groups should be heterogeneous (the more diverse the better). They typically have four or five members. When students are assigned to a core group, they know they'll be meeting with these same students for an extended period of time (e.g., a semester or a full school year). Johnson and Johnson (1989) recommend core groups as a way of ensuring psychological health and social competencies, as well as friendships. Indeed, many students will do their homework because they do not want to let their fellow core-team members down. The agenda for core-group meetings includes time for: 1) discussing the academic tasks assigned to each member and the strategies for achieving these tasks; 2) taking attendance or collecting permission slips for field trips; and 3) providing personal support, such as listening as each person speaks about their progress on assignments or their experiences at home or in other classes. Some teachers use core groups only for "show and tell" and "current events," which limits the students' time together to only 6 minutes (1 minute for each of 6 members in a group).

Through the use of direct instruction, modeling, and role playing, core groups can be used to explicitly teach students how to establish and maintain a social support group or a network of friends (see Thousand & Villa, 1990). The students rehearse such skills as initiating a conversation and making nonverbal behavior consistent with verbal behavior.

Formal Groups   Teachers assign students to heterogeneous groups for specified time periods (typically 3–4 weeks) that last until a task is completed. Each formal learning group comprises two or three classmates who work together to ensure that each of them achieves the specific learning objectives.

Temporary Groups   Teachers assign students to groups of two or three for 1 or 2 class periods so that they can confirm each other's understanding of the material and help each other to expand their knowledge of concepts. This technique is especially helpful following lectures, films, field trips, and other activities that involve many potential distractions.

Setting the Task and Goal Structure

There are three basic ways that teachers can organize students to allow them to accomplish their academic tasks cooperatively: goal interdependence, resource interdependence, and reward interdependence (see, Putnam, chap. 2 this volume). Students know that they have two basic jobs to accomplish during any cooperative learning lesson. First, they are individually accountable for making sure that they achieve the instructional objectives, especially when some individuals have unique items to learn (e.g., different spelling words or math facts). Second, they are responsible for maintaining positive relationships with each group member in case they have to work together in the future. Students learn various effective team behaviors while helping each other, such as using each other's names, making and praising contributions, summarizing answers, checking to make sure that everyone agrees, and probing for deeper understanding.

Monitoring Individual and Group Interactions

While students work together to achieve their academic objectives, the teachers are present, but not intrusive unless necessary. But they do not leave the room for a coffee break and they do not sit at their desks correcting papers. There are two vital functions that teachers actually look forward to when students work in groups. First, the teachers plan to eavesdrop, to listen and watch for the cues that tell them that their students are working cooperatively. These cues include huddling (students putting their heads together) and buzzing (referring to the sound of students' voices as they talk about the assignment). Second, teachers move from one group to another to note the frequency and quality of the cooperative skills that the students are using. This information helps teachers to decide whether interventions are needed. During the evaluation of a cooperative lesson, frequencies and feedback examples can be shared with students to show them the relationship between their level of achievement on the academic task and the quality of their cooperative/collaborative skills.

Teacher-Monitored Processes   In teacher-monitored processes, the teacher tallies frequencies of participation in predetermined categories (e.g., asking questions, praising, confirming understanding) for each student.

Student-Monitored Processes   In student-monitored processes, one student in each group tallies the frequencies of participation in predetermined categories that are considered important for task achievement (e.g., paraphrasing a team member's statements to show listening skills, or encouraging team members to contribute).

Intervening To Solve Academic and Social Problems

Students who work in cooperative learning groups may have specific challenges to face, such as situations in which one member does all the work, or one member refuses to work, or some members do not know how to do the work. Teachers can step in to intervene to help the group solve either the academic or the social problem. Sometimes teachers turn the problem back over to the group and return a short time later to check on the solutions. In other cases, teachers ask the entire class to assist in generating solutions. The basic idea is that problems are not something to be hidden or denied. Indeed, a problem often becomes the basis for future lessons. If the problem is related to misunderstanding an aspect of the academic subject, teachers use it as an opportunity for additional study. In fact students themselves will sometimes request additional work or resources to help them.

Evaluating Cooperative Learning Lessons

Teachers can give immediate feedback on the academic aspects of the lesson by collecting the completed work and correcting it while students discuss how well they worked together and what improvements they need to make for future work sessions. (Notice that if there are five groups, for example, a teacher only needs to correct five papers instead of 30.) Another technique used by teachers is to randomly select individuals to share their groups' ideas. This technique has the added advantage of helping to ensure individual accountability. When teachers want all students in the group to complete a specific assignment, then only one random paper from each group is collected and graded. Each paper presumably represents what everyone in the group has contributed and, thus, whatever grade the chosen paper receives is recorded for each group member. This technique is helpful in encouraging students to take comprehensive notes.

In addition to sharing the results of their academic work, students are also evaluated on their cooperative skills. The teacher's anecdotal records and tallies can be discussed with individual groups, as well as with the class as a whole. Plans can then be made for what each individual, each group, and the whole class will practice for future cooperative lessons.

Redesigning Cooperative Learning Lessons

The planning format for cooperative learning lessons is naturally a discovery process. The lesson plan worksheet shown in Figure 1, which is adapted from Johnson, Johnson, and Holubec, (1987) is a helpful aid in generating lesson plans, noting results, and making changes. One advantage of this format is that it displays, at a glance, the eight steps of the teacher's role. A disadvantage, however, is that it may not provide enough detail (for more detail, see the planning format recommended by Villa and Thousand in Chapter 4 of this volume). Make sure, however, that you schedule time to celebrate the changes in students' academic and social competence, even as new lessons to ameliorate deficiencies are invented, implemented, evaluated, and redesigned.

SOME EXAMPLES

The following examples of cooperative learning lessons have been designed by teachers for students with especially challenging educational needs. They illustrate many of the curricular and instructional adaptations described above.

Case 1.   Joy Wilcox, an experienced elementary school teacher, collaborated with a paraprofessional, a University professor, and a research assistant to include a nonverbal 8-year-old girl with severe disabilities in a 1st-grade general education classroom (Wilcox, Sbardellati, & Nevin, 1987). Debbie became a successful member of the class for daily story time, the morning academic period, lunch, and recess. Cooperative lessons were designed to incorporate her IEP objectives (e.g., following directions, color naming) into the 1st-grade curriculum. Over a 9-day cycle of lessons, the teacher was particularly adept at frequently reassigning

COOPERATIVE LEARNING LESSON FORMAT

Curriculum area: _____

IEP objectives of students with disabilities: _____

Adaptations for students with disabilities: _____

Academic objective(s): _____

Collaborative skill objective(s): _____

Group size: _____

Who will be assigned to each group? _____

Materials: _____

Time required: _____

Plan the lesson (creating goal/resource/reward interdependence):

Academic task: _____

_____

Criteria for success: _____

_____

50

Positive interdependence: _____

Individual accountability: _____

Expected cooperative behaviors: _____

Monitoring will be done by: ☐ Teacher ☐ Students

Monitoring will focus on: ☐ Whole class ☐ Group ☐ Student

Collaborative behaviors to be monitored: _____

Closure (How will students summarize what they have learned? How will feedback on group performance be given? How will students plan their future use of specified social skills?): _____

Results: _____

Suggested changes for future lessons: _____

Figure 1. Lesson plan worksheet

groups so that Debbie worked with every member of the class. Students practiced the cooperative skills of sharing materials, helping others, and praising other team members for their efforts. The teacher was happy that the results went far beyond expectations. Not only did Debbie increase her rate of initiation of interactions with her classmates, her classmates also increased their initiations of interactions with her. These interactions were typical of friendships—that is, Debbie was not always the "helpee," but often served as "helper" to other students. Initiated and reciprocated interactions also increased during recess and lunch. Debbie's mother reported that Debbie became more verbal at home; even though her vocabulary was difficult to understand, she seemed to have more of a desire to communicate.

Case 2.   Mary Kay Monley (1989) developed a science lesson for a general education class in order to include Bobby, who was visually impaired and nonverbal. In a lesson in which the objective was for all students to identify different fruits by their seeds (color, size, shape, and number), each group was to complete a poster and, as a group, present it to the rest of the class. Posters were expected to include four or five different fruits and their seeds. Bobby's objective was to tactually explore each fruit and to stay with the group. The objective was explained to the students, and they were asked what other things Bobby could do to be part of the group's activities. The students suggested that Bobby paste some materials on to the poster instead of drawing them. Once all the groups had completed and corrected their posters as necessary, each made and ate a fruit salad.

Case 3.   A 10th-grade math teacher who had referred several students with behavior disorders for special services collaborated with two consulting teachers and a university professor to design cooperative lessons to decrease the students' maladaptive behaviors and increase their math achievement (Nevin, Polewski, & Skieber, 1987). The teacher started with an instructional unit on decimals. He gave pre- and post-test feedback on achievement and students' attitudes toward the cooperative learning lessons. The unit was completed in four 45-minute periods; each period included a short lecture or chalkboard demonstration by the teacher, followed by time for students to work cooperatively in groups of four. The teacher monitored the groups, tallying inappropriate and disruptive behaviors as well as academic achievement. Daily feedback was provided to each group about their accuracy and about how well they worked together. Results showed that all the students (including those who were disruptive) improved: pre-test scores ranged from 0 to 5 correct, with a mean of 1.8, while on the posttest, all students achieved a perfect score of 12. In addition, the results of the attitude test showed that students were favorably disposed toward working in groups. The most dramatic effects were in the decrease of inappropriate and disruptive behaviors. Before heterogeneous cooperative learning, students had averaged over 10 disruptions per period, but during the cooperative learning lessons, they averaged fewer than three.

Case 4.   A social studies lesson for an eighth grader who had limited reading and spelling skills and memory deficits was collaboratively developed by Karen Noone (1990) and the teacher. They adapted the curriculum (learning about the countries of Africa) to address the student's IEP objectives (increasing memory skills). The teacher asked each of six groups of four students to develop a memory aid, or mnemonic, to represent each of three sets of African countries being studied. The student with memory deficits was held accountable for one of the sets (a reduced assignment). All of the groups were successful in creating mnemonics that enabled them to remember both the names of the nations and their locations, for example "MATLE" (for the contiguous North African states of Morocco, Algeria, Tunisia, Libya, and Egypt) and "My Mother Never Cooked Soup Every Night During Supper" for the contiguous middle states of Mauritania, Morai, Niger, Chad, Sudan, Ethiopia, and North Djibouti).

SOME PRACTICAL ADVICE

There are several things that educators can do to make the transition to cooperative learning a smooth one.

1.   *Join or start a Cooperative Learning Study Group.*   Make sure it's heterogeneous—the more diverse the better. Structure it so that each person has a chance to give and receive feedback about using cooperative learning in his or her classroom and to practice collaborative skills that a teacher might not feel comfortable enough to demonstrate. Set it up so that it is normal for new lessons to be invented when a planned lesson doesn't seem to be working out the way it was intended. Chapter 3 of this volume, by Villa and Thousand, provides information and advice on working on cooperative teaching teams.

2.   *Learn to ask for help in a thousand different ways, even when you think you don't need it.*   In other words, you don't have to be in a crisis situation to ask for feedback. If a lesson isn't working out as intended, stop. Ask students for feedback on what went wrong in the lesson or advice on how it can be improved. Ask a colleague, supervisor, another member of the IEP team, or the parent of a student in your room (or another teacher's room) to observe your cooperative lessons and give you feedback.

3.   *Volunteer to observe another teacher's cooperative lessons.*   Be hon-

est about what you notice. If you carry some of this teacher's methods into your own cooperative lessons, let the other teacher know how he or she influenced you. Imitation, after all, is the sincerest form of flattery.

4. *Keep a diary/log/journal of your cooperative learning lesson plans for at least 6 months—and read it.*   Notice (be honest) what's working and what's not. Be reflective (rather than judgmental). Do not grade yourself (e.g., 7 out of 8 steps implemented = A). Instead, celebrate every time you conduct a cooperative lesson. Celebrate every outcome (intended or unintended). Treat "failures" as opportunities to invent new lessons.

5. *Give yourself lots of gifts, especially the gift of time.*   It can take as long as 2 even 3 years to master cooperative learning methodology to the "routine-use" level, on the plane at which academic and collaborative skills can be integrated spontaneously in any lesson (see Johnson et al., 1987). Consider also the gift of Practicality. Start with a single lesson, then add at least one cooperative lesson per week, then adapt a curriculum unit.

6. *Be prepared to celebrate unexpected, unintended outcomes.*   Teachers who have used cooperative learning report subtle as well as obvious changes in their students. Yes, achievement changes: measures on standardized and teacher-prepared tests show increased performance. Attitudes toward school, the subject, and the teacher will also change. Students with differences show improvement. And be prepared for changes in yourself!

> Cooperation is more than an instructional procedure. The data supporting cooperation is as strong for adults as it is for children and adolescents. . . . Applying cooperation at one level prepares the person for participating in it at the next level. Teaching students how to work cooperatively prepares teachers to collaborate with their peers. (Johnson & Johnson, 1988, p. 10)

CONCLUDING COMMENTS

There is a growing network of teachers who have collaborated with educational specialists and parents of students with disabilities to adapt curriculum and instruction so that cooperative learning lessons can be successfully implemented in inclusive classrooms. Curricular adaptations include chronological age-appropriate curriculum objectives and materials, functional equivalents, integrated services, task analyses, overlapping objectives, different response modes, and adjustments of evaluation systems. Instructional adaptations include various methods to adjust group size and membership (core groups, formal groups, and temporary groups), setting the task and goal structure (reward, resource, or goal interdependence), monitoring individual and group interactions, intervening to help students solve academic and social problems, and evaluating students' achievements and social interactions.

The case-study examples in this chapter show how elementary and secondary school teachers, in collaboration with others, can adapt curricula and instruction to create cooperative lessons that include students with disabilities. Teachers and students alike simply need to be inventive and flexible in their efforts to ensure academic and social progress.

REFERENCES

Benjamin, S. (1989). An ideascape for education: What futurists recommend. *Educational Leadership, 47*(1), 8–14.

Cosden, M. (1989). Cooperative groups and microcomputer instruction. *The Pointer, 33*(2), 21–26.

Fink, C. (1990). Cooperating with computers. *Preventing School Failure, 34*(4), 20–24.

Giangreco, M., Cloninger, C., & Iverson, V. (1990). C.O.A.C.H.—*Cayuga-Onondaga Assessment for Children with Handicaps* (6th ed.) (pp. 36–39). Stillwater: Oklahoma State University, National Clearinghouse of Rehabilitative Training Materials.

Giangreco, M.F., & Putnam, J.W. (1991). Supporting the education of students with severe disabilities in regular education environments. In L.H. Meyer, C.A. Peck, & L. Brown (Eds.), *Critical issues in the lives of people with severe disabilities* (pp. 245–270). Baltimore: Paul H. Brookes Publishing Co.

Idol, L., Nevin, A., & Paolucci-Whitcomb, P. (1986). *Models of curriculum based assessment.* Austin, TX: PRO-ED.

Johnson, D., & Johnson, R. (1987). *Learning together and alone: Cooperation, competition, and individualization* (2nd ed.). Englewood Cliffs, NJ: Prentice Hall.

Johnson, D., & Johnson, R. (1988). *Cooperative classrooms, cooperative schools.* (Monograph available from Cooperative Learning Center, 202 Pattee Hall, University of Minnesota, Minneapolis, MN 55455).

Johnson, D., & Johnson, R. (1989). Base groups: What are they? *The Cooperative Link, 6*(1), 2–3. (Newsletter available from Cooperative Learning Center, 202 Pattee Hall, University of Minnesota, Minneapolis, MN 55455).

Johnson, D., Johnson, R., & Holubec, E. (1987). *Structuring cooperative learning: The 1987 lesson plan handbook.* Edina, MN: Interaction Book Company.

Monley, M.K. (1989). *Cooperative group lesson: Fruit seeds.* (Report completed in partial fulfillment of requirements for Professor J. Thousand, EDSP 322). Burlington: University of Vermont.

Nevin, A., Polewski, C., & Skieber, E. (1987). The impact of cooperative learning in a regular classroom. *The Pointer, 28,* 19–21.

Noone, K. (1990). *Locating African countries.* (Report completed in partial fulfillment of requirements for Professor J. Thousand, EDSP 322). Burlington: University of Vermont.

Putnam, J. (1990). Curriculum adaptations for students with disabilities in cooperative groups. *Cooperative Learning, 12*(1), 3–4.

Slavin, R. (1990). *Cooperative learning: Theory, research, and practice.* Englewood Cliffs, NJ: Prentice Hall.

Thousand, J., & Villa, R. (1990). Strategies for educating learners with severe handicaps within their local home schools and communities. *Focus on Exceptional Children, 23*(3), 1–25.

Wilcox, J., Sbardellati, E., & Nevin, A. (1987). Cooperative learning aids integration. *Teaching Exceptional Children,* 61–63.

4

Redefining the Role
of the Special Educator
and Other Support Personnel

RICHARD A. VILLA
AND JACQUELINE S. THOUSAND

Cooperative group learning models
are the most carefully researched educational approach for promoting
heterogeneous student grouping (Johnson & Johnson, 1987; Slavin,
1984, 1987, 1989). These models are gaining increased popularity and
acceptance as school personnel recognize the need to foster students' social and interpersonal skill development and to create heterogeneous
school communities that reflect and prepare students for the "real world"
of the twenty-first century—an ever-changing global community in
which diversity (e.g., cultural, racial, ethnic, linguistic, economic, and
ability) will be the norm.

Both authors of this chapter devote a great deal of time to training
administrators, classroom teachers, and support personnel (e.g., special
educators, guidance personnel, speech and language specialists, compensatory education personnel) in cooperative learning methods. We
have discovered that many school personnel who have a history of working in isolation (e.g., in self-contained general education, or in separate
class settings for atypical students) are mystified by the idea of collaborat-

This chapter was simultaneously prepared for publication in this volume and in Thousand, J.S., Villa, R.A., & Nevin, A. (Eds.). (In press). *Creativity and collaborative learning:
A practical guide to empowering students and teachers*. Baltimore: Paul H. Brookes Publishing
Co. It appears here, in slightly edited and revised format, by permission of the authors and
publisher.

ing to educate a more diverse group of learners through interactive processes such as cooperative learning. They, as well as their students, are full of questions regarding their new role as partners in teaching and learning within cooperative structures.

The questions most frequently posed by special educators, who are accustomed to delivering student support primarily through pull-out services outside of the general education classroom, include the following:

What is my role, versus that of the classroom teacher in cooperative learning experiences?

Do I go into the general education classroom with the students whom I serve in order to support them in their cooperative learning groups?

How do I ensure that the students whom I serve are successful members of cooperative learning groups in the general education environment?

Do I sit with the students that I support as a member of a student-learning group?

Am I to interact with other students in the classroom?

The questions most often asked by classroom teachers are:

How do I most effectively work with a special education professional or other support person during cooperative group learning activities?

What are the benefits of having another educator in the classroom?

Who plans for and evaluates which students?

How do the students whom I support fit into cooperative learning groups?

Students ask:

Which one is my teacher?

Whom do I ask for help?

Whose rules and discipline procedures apply to me?

If the special education teacher helps me, will people think that I'm a "special education" student?

Will both teachers want to talk so much that we won't have time to work in our groups?

All of these questions reflect the confusion of both educators and students regarding their roles when collaborative and cooperative teaching and learning arrangements are introduced in order to maximize student success.

A primary purpose of this chapter is to illustrate how classroom teachers and support personnel can effectively share expertise and responsibility to promote not only the learning and collaborative skill development of their students, but their own professional and interpersonal growth as well. We first offer the rationale for professional partnership in the design and delivery of cooperative learning instruction and define a *cooperative education team*. We then describe strategies to reduce role confusion among classroom teachers and support personnel through teachers' systematic analyses and distributions of instructional responsibilities (i.e., planning, teaching, and evaluating student performance) followed by examples of cooperative education teams in action and tips for optimizing team effectiveness. The two forms that appear at the end of the chapter, which the reader has permission to photocopy, can be of great help in conducting team meetings and in planning cooperative lessons.

WHY CREATE COOPERATIVE EDUCATION TEAMS?

Modeling What We Preach

The integration of professionals within a school system is a prerequisite to the successful integration of students. We cannot ask our students to do those things which we as professionals are unwilling to do. (Harris, 1987, p. 1)

Conventional wisdom suggests that a primary learning method for both children and adults is the observation of behaviors displayed by role models. A critical duty of the teacher, then, in preparing students for the cooperative workplace and for the society of the twenty-first century, is to model cooperative teaching; thus, students learn through observation how two or more people coordinate instructional, behavior management, and student-evaluation activities. Adult modeling of the same behavior reinforces the message that cooperative behavior is a norm that extends beyond student life to adulthood and life-long success. Adult modeling also increases the likelihood that students will value and cooperate with teachers to create a collaborative classroom culture.

Two Heads Are Better than One

Having worked extensively in public schools with classroom teachers and specialists who regularly collaborate with each other in instruction and who employ cooperative learning methods in their instructional routines, we have found that these educators experience creative thinking and problemsolving outcomes (Thousand & Villa, 1990) similar to those experienced by students who learn in heterogeneous cooperative groups (Johnson & Johnson, 1991). In particular, collaborating teachers are able to generate new conceptualizations and novel solutions to the daily challenges presented by a diverse student population through the synergistic processes of *collective induction* (i.e., inducing general principles together that no single person could induce individually) and *process gain* (i.e., generating new ideas through group interaction that would not be generated by a person working alone).

A primary purpose of assembling a cooperative education team is to increase the potential for individualizing instruction while enabling all students to be educated with their peers. With multiple instructors, the teacher–student ratio is higher, which allows for more immediate and accurate diagnosis of, and intervention in response to, individual student academic and social needs. Instructors also have a greater opportunity to capitalize on the diverse, unique, and specialized knowledge, skills, and instructional approaches of team members who have had different training and experiences.

Professional Growth and Peer Support

There are many possible stereotypic responses to the question, "What do general educators have to offer special educators, and vice versa?" One is that general education teachers possess content mastery in any number of topical areas, from reading and writing to the sciences, whereas special educators have knowledge of specific techniques for remediating or accelerating learning in more basic skill areas, such as mathematics or reading. Another response might be that general educators have the experience and skill to manage large groups of learners, whereas special educators have the skill to design individual behavior-management plans and to teach social skills that enhance self-management and social acceptability within the classroom. Whatever the response, it is likely that educators will acknowledge that each person in the school community possesses unique talents and perspectives that, when pooled, create a richer learning environment for adults as well as for children. In other words, in cooperative education teams, teachers may experience professional growth that cannot be attained through formal coursework.

Research on staff development highlights the importance of educators having frequent opportunities to observe models of new instructional methods, and to receive coaching and feedback during their efforts to replicate and personalize the new technique (Showers, Joyce, & Bennett, 1987). Cooperative education teams are natural settings for modeling and analysis to occur in. Of course, "peer coaching" (Cummings, 1985, p. 1) both requires and promotes a high level of trust and mutual interdependence among cooperating teachers. Such an interdependent support system for obtaining feedback is necessary to help teachers ensure the integrity and continued improvement of their use of cooperative learning and to sustain their interest in doing so (Johnson, Johnson, Holubec, & Roy, 1984). Johnson and his colleagues advocate the networking of cooperative education teams through a school-wide professional support group to ensure the long-term continued practice of cooperative methods. In this larger support group, teams may share ideas, lessons, and successes, and may solve individual and mutual problems that occur when using cooperative learning methods. They can also structure reciprocal observation and coaching opportunities to improve one another's competence in using cooperative learning procedures.

Support personnel such as special educators who provide technical assistance to several teachers are a very important resource for spreading cooperative learning throughout a school. By offering to teach other teachers' classes, they can model cooperative learning methods for both teachers and students. Support personnel may also "free up" other members of their cooperative education teams so that they too can model in other classrooms.

WHAT IS A COOPERATIVE EDUCATION TEAM?

A *cooperative education team* is an instructional arrangement of two or more people in the school and/or greater community who share cooperative learning planning, instruction, and evaluation responsibilities for the same students on a regular basis for an extended period of time. Teams may vary in size from two to six members. They should vary in composition as well, comprising any possible combination of support personnel (e.g., special educators, speech-language pathologists, guidance counselors, health professionals), instructional assistants, student teachers, community volunteers [e.g., parents, members of local "foster grandparent" programs] teachers, and students themselves) (Thousand & Villa, 1990).

Members of an effective cooperative education team practice the same critical elements that they structure for their students' cooperative learning groups. Specifically, members: 1) have frequent face-to-face interactions, 2) structure a positive "we are all in this together" sense of interdependence, 3) hold one another individually accountable for agreed-upon responsibilities, 4) practice small-group interpersonal skills, and 5) periodically assess and discuss their instructional and interpersonal effectiveness.

Face-to-Face Interaction

The questions posed most often by newly formed cooperative education teams are those that have to do with scheduling time for face-to-face interactions. When and how often does the team meet? How much time, during or outside of school hours, will team meetings take? Of the support personnel (e.g., special educators, speech-language pathologists,

Chapter 1 instructors, teaching assistants), who will be regular members of the team? When should other people who support students in the classroom (e.g., guidance counselors, health professionals, "outside" consultants, therapists) attend meetings? What means will members of the team use to relay information quickly among themselves when a formal planning meeting is not scheduled (e.g., a communication log, an electronic bulletin board on the classroom computer, "Post-It" notes)?

Questions about face-to-face interaction should be settled through team members discussing and collaboratively agreeing on answers. Time must be arranged for team members to not only plan cooperative lessons, but also to evaluate the effectiveness of the lessons as well. The need for face-to-face interactions also affects team size. The literature on student cooperative learning arrangements suggests that there should be no more than five or six members in a group (Johnson et al., 1984); the same size limitation holds for adult teams if each member is to have adequate "air time" during meetings.

Positive Interdependence

In most North American schools, teachers, whether general educators or special support personnel, are still expected to work alone and independently of one another. This expectation determines not only how teachers behave, but also how they think about the students for whom they are assigned responsibility ("These students ['general' or 'special'] are mine and, therefore, my primary or sole responsibility," or "Those students ['special' or 'general'] are not mine, and therefore of little instructional concern to me.").

For cooperative education teams, positive interdependence changes this. Positive interdependence involves the recognition among team members that no one person can effectively address the diverse educational, social, and psychological needs of a heterogeneous group of students (i.e., all students become both yours *and* mine). It encourages members of the teams to feel that they are all responsible for the education of their students through the pooling of their diverse skills, knowledge, and material resources. The strategies that teams may employ to create feelings of positive interdependence include distributing and rotating "classroom leadership" and decisionmaking powers (i.e., the who, what, where, when, why, and how of designing and delivering cooperative lessons) among all members of the team, and regularly celebrating the team's successes in designing and conducting lessons (e.g., including "positive statements" as the first agenda item for all planning and evaluation meetings and sharing lesson outcomes with other teachers, parents, administrators, or members of the general community).

A cooperative education team "does everything that a 'normal' teacher would do except that now there are two or more people doing it"

(N. Keller, personal communication, March 17, 1989); in other words, one job is divided between two or more people. The key is the implicit recognition that numerous decisions are made about how the formerly separate "classroom leadership" responsbilities and powers of team members are redistributed and readjusted over time. Some of the questions that team members must jointly answer are presented in Table 1. Tough decisions have to be made at times, but the professional and personal growth that may result from making such decisions is an invaluable outcome not easily achieved in public schools today.

Individual Accountability

Collaboration, as illustrated by teaching teams, has the potential to increase teachers' accountability. In a collaborative school, teachers "monitor one another's performance, set limits on one another's behavior, and

Table 1.   Questions that members of a cooperative learning teaching team must answer to distribute leadership responsibilities among team members

1. Who will plan the academic content of the lesson?
2. How will the lesson be presented and explained? Will one person teach the social skills, another the academic material, and other(s) assist in observing, intervening, and evaluating with student learning groups? Or will all members share in the instruction, monitoring, and processing?
3. Who will adapt the materials, instructional procedures, and performance expectations for individual students?
4. Who will evaluate which students? Will team members collaborate in evaluating all students' performances, or will each team member be primarily responsible for evaluating a group of students?
5. How will the paperwork for students eligible for special education be managed?
6. Who will decide on the intervention procedures for disruptive student behavior? Who will carry out the procedures? How will consistency be ensured?
7. How will team members arrange to share and enhance their skills? Will they observe one another and practice "peer coaching?"
8. Will team members rotate teaching and student monitoring and processing responsibilities? How often will these responsibilities rotate? How will the decision be made to shift these responsibilities?
9. Who will have the authority to make on-the-spot adjustments to the lesson? How and when during the lesson will decisionmakers confer to agree upon needed adjustments?
10. Who will communicate with parents and administrators?
11. How will the decision be made to expand or contract the team membership?
12. How will an equitable balance of work and decisionmaking power be maintained among team members?

take responsibility for helping their colleagues to improve" (Smith, 1987, p. 6). The natural consequence of structuring cooperative education teams is the introduction of additional "eyes" into the learning environment and opportunities for team members to observe and assess one another relative to their agreed-upon planning, teaching, monitoring, and evaluation responsibilities.

There is no question that working as a team reduces the autonomy and freedom enjoyed by teachers when they function independently of one another (Skrtic, 1991). However, a primary purpose of teaming structures is to maximize the instructional performance of each individual through the modeling, coaching, and feedback that teammates provide (Johnson et al., 1984). The possible loss of freedom that teaming implies is balanced by the freedom of not being solely responsible for students' learning; the potential for more effectively dealing with an increasingly diverse student population; and the sense of belonging, as well as fun, that accompanies successful, creative, shared problemsolving (Glasser, 1986; Parnes, 1981, 1988).

Small-Group Social Skills

Just because two or more people call themselves a team is no guarantee that they will interact cooperatively. For an adult or student team to collaborate effectively, members must possess and use small-group interpersonal skills. Unfortunately, few teachers and support personnel who are members of cooperative education teams have had the same opportunity as their students to receive instruction and practice in small-group skills. As a consequence, newly formed teams will include people who have never before been required to demonstrate collaborative skills.

The most effective teams are those whose members are able to maintain equity and parity by arriving at decisions through a consensual (i.e., all members agree) rather than a democratic (i.e., a majority of members agree) process. To behave in a consensual fashion, however, requires the acquisition and mastery of a great many small-group social skills, and these skills cannot be mastered overnight. The four levels of skills that team members need to demonstrate in order for group growth to occur are: 1) initial trust-building skills (forming skills); 2) communication and leadership skills that help members to manage and organize team activities so that tasks are completed and relationships are maintained (functioning skills); 3) skills necessary to stimulate creative problemsolving and decisionmaking and to allow deeper comprehension of unfamiliar or confusing information (formulating skills); and 4) skills needed to manage controversy and conflict of opinions and interests, to search for more information (e.g., obtain technical assistance from outside the team), and to stimulate the revision and refinement of ideas (fermenting skills) (Johnson et al., 1984; Thousand & Villa, 1992).

Of course, small-group interpersonal skills can be learned by adults as well as children; and learning them is no different from learning any other skill. It requires opportunities for team members to: 1) see the need for the skill, 2) learn how and when to use it, 3) practice using it, and 4) receive feedback on how well they are using it (Johnson et al., 1984). A major challenge in the early stages of cooperative education teams is deciding how to acquire these small-group collaborative skills. One direct method is to arrange for training and guided practice as part of an ongoing inservice agenda. An indirect and natural method, one recommended by David and Roger Johnson, is for teachers to simply begin teaching social skills to students as part of cooperative learning lessons. In this way, through the process of teaching, teachers acquire the same skills as the students and develop an understanding of the importance of these skills to any team's functioning (Brandt, 1987). A third method is to allow time for team members to evaluate their instructional and interpersonal effectiveness as a regular part of planning meetings.

Evaluating Team Effectiveness

As already noted, research on staff development highlights the importance of structuring frequent opportunities for teachers to evaluate and receive feedback on the innovative practices that they are attempting (Showers et al., 1987). This is particularly true for cooperative education teams whose members are likely to have had little previous experience in co-planning, co-teaching, or using small-group interpersonal skills. The final critical element for team success involves the regular scheduling of time for the team to evaluate instructional and interpersonal effectiveness and to set social-growth goals for individuals and for the group as a whole. Outside observers (e.g., a colleague from another cooperative education team, a supervisor with knowledge and experience in cooperative learning, guidance personnel with knowledge of social-skill development and group interaction) may be invited to observe planning meetings or cooperative lessons and to share their observations as part of the team's professional-development activities or as an intervention when the team is having trouble functioning.

HOW DO MEMBERS OF THE EDUCATION TEAM PLAN, CONDUCT, AND EVALUATE COOPERATIVE LEARNING EXPERIENCES?

Cooperative learning may be incorporated into the culture of the classroom in three ways: 1) through *formal* lessons and learning groups that are more structured and stay together until a task is completed (e.g., a group of four completes a week-long science unit and ensures that all members master the assigned information); 2) through *informal* learning groups that are transient and less structured (e.g., "Turn to your neighbor and share with one another our three lessons"); and 3) through *base groups*, in which students have long-term (e.g., semester- or year-long) responsibility for providing one another with peer support and long-term accountability (Johnson & Johnson, 1991).

Once a cooperative education team understands how to structure formal cooperative lessons, the other two types of cooperative learning experiences can (and should) be added to the curriculum. Clearly, formal cooperative lessons require the greatest degree of coordination and mutual decisionmaking among members of the cooperative education team. Hence, this section addresses the roles and decisions required of members of a cooperative education team as they develop, teach, and evaluate formal cooperative learning experiences. Of course, what team members learn though these experiences will also better enable them to use informal and base groups.

Planning Cooperative Learning Lessons

As with all effective instruction, planning is the key to the successful delivery of a cooperative group lesson. In planning a lesson, the first team task is to agree on and clearly specify the academic and social skill objectives. The second is to make certain decisions regarding face-to-face interaction (which students will be in which groups, the size of each group, the arrangement of the room), how students will be made interdependent, how academic and social skills will be taught and monitored, and how feedback on task and social skill performance will be provided to individual students. The cooperative group lesson plan that appears at the end of this chapter shows the diverse factors that a cooperative education team must consider when constructing a formal lesson. The team must clearly specify the academic and social skill objectives and make the series of decisions regarding face-to-face interaction, the structuring of positive interdependence among students, social skill instruction and monitoring, and reviewing with students their task and social skill performance. A great number of these decisions also require the team to agree on who will do what—for example, how responsibility for direct instruction will be distributed among team members. The questions the team should consider when deciding how the role of teacher should be distributed among team members are presented in Table 1. Listed below are some additional questions that relate to the individualization of instruction for students:

Will there be different academic objectives, materials, or performance criteria for some learners? Who will select the objectives, measure student performance, and review the students' performance with them?

Will there be different social skill objectives or performance criteria for
some learners? Who will select the objectives, measure student performance, and review these students' performance with them?

Will some students receive pre-teaching in academic or social skill areas?
When will this pre-teaching occur? Who will conduct the instruction?

Will differences in academic or social objectives for different students be
communicated to the class or the group to which the student be-
longs? When will this communication occur? Who will communicate the information? What is the rationale for communicating or
not communicating this information? Is confidentiality an issue that
should be addressed with families of students eligible for special
education?

***Creating Positive Interdependence Through a Structured
Team Meeting Process***   Like student cooperative learning experiences, planning meetings of a cooperative education team must be structured to promote a feeling of positive interdependence among team
members (Thousand & Villa, 1992). Positive interdependence may be
created through a division of labor during team meetings as well as during the delivery of the lessons themselves. It is recommended that team
members rotate, from one meeting to the next, different leadership roles
that promote either the completion of work or the maintenance of relationships among members. With this structure, the team has as many
leaders as members, and the message is communicated that no single
person has all of the expertise, authority, materials, or information resources needed to accomplish the team's goals.

Numerous task (e.g., timekeeper, recorder) and relationship (e.g.,
observer, encourager) roles have been prescribed and defined by various
authors (Glickman, 1990; Johnson et al., 1984; Thousand & Villa, 1992).
Exactly which roles a team decides to use during a meeting depends on
the nature of the lesson being planned and the level of interpersonal skill
development among team members. For example, when conflict and
controversy are expected, there may be a need for a "conflict recognizer"
to identify emerging conflicts and to signal the team to stop and assess
whether the steps of conflict resolution should be initiated. A "harmonizer" may also be needed to help conciliate differences by looking for
ways to reduce tension through humor and nonjudgemental explanations. A "praiser" is important when a team has become negligent in regularly affirming the contributions of members. When team discussions
become dominated by particular participants, an "equalizer" can regu-
late the flow of communication by ensuring that all members have equal
access to "air time" and by encouraging quiet members to participate.

Any social skill can be transformed into a role to be practiced by, and
rotated among, team members. Two roles recently invented by school-

based collaborative teams are the "but watcher" and "jargon buster" roles. The job of the "but watcher" is to help team members to defer judgement during creative idea-generating or problemsolving periods by monitoring and signaling a member's use of blocking, oppositional, or judgmental language, such as, "Yes, but that won't work because . . . " A "jargon buster" has the job of signaling whenever a specialized term may not be understood. The jargon user must then define the term or use an analogous term that everyone is familiar with. This role is very important for cooperative education teams that include special educators or other support personnel professionals who may commonly use jargon to describe their work and ideas. The jargon buster prevents team members who are unfamiliar with particular terms from feeling intimidated or less than equal. He or she also establishes that it is perfectly all right not to know everything. Once team members are familiar with the meaning of jargon, the terms may be used by the group to enhance its efficiency and to promote a feeling of interdependence. A common language tends to increase communication and to build a team's sense of identity and spirit.

The Team Meeting Worksheet   The team meeting worksheet that appears at the end of the chapter has proven to be an effective outline for promoting accountability among team members with regard to attendance and the equitable distribution of work during and after planning meetings (Thousand & Villa, 1992). The worksheet also ensures that attention is given to the other elements of the collaborative teaming process (i.e., face-to-face interaction, positive interdependence, collaborative skill performance, evaluation). The worksheet is a valuable guide at team meetings. In order to emphasize individual accountability for meeting attendance, names of present, late, and absent members are recorded on the worksheet. Names of others who are not at the meeting, but who need to be informed of team outcomes (e.g., extended team members who may be involved in subsequent lessons, administrators or other teachers in the school interested in cooperative groupings) are also noted; this alerts the team of who may need to be given information on the outcomes of planning. The distribution of leadership responsibilities is prompted by the list of possible roles included on the worksheet and the indication that roles are to be assigned in advance of the next meeting. This ensures that the people in roles such as timekeeper and recorder will bring the necessary materials with them. Advance role assignment also prompts team members to rotate roles from one meeting to the next.

Notice that the team is prompted to create the agenda for the next meeting before it disbands. If all members are informed (at the meeting and through the minutes) of the date, location, purpose, and time of the next meeting, then accountability is ensured. This also encourages members to participate in the next meeting; people take more interest in events and objectives that they themselves have helped to plan.

The "examination of the agenda" section of the worksheet reveals that incorporated into all meetings are: 1) time limits for each agenda item; 2) a time to celebrate the things that went well in the cooperative lessons just taught, as well as other positive educationally related events experienced since the last meeting; and 3) a time, midway and at the end of the meeting, to review members' use of collaborative skills and their progress toward completion of the lesson. The empty numbered spaces listed on the agenda worksheet represent the actual content of each meeting—the subtasks that contribute to the team's achievement of its overall goals, including successful lesson design. Although the agenda proposed at the end of a meeting guides the construction of the actual agenda of the team's next planning meeting, it must be remembered that many events can occur between meetings. Consequently, the actual agenda items should be modified at the beginning of each meeting to reflect the intervening events.

Promoting Equity Through the Planning Process   The ultimate outcome of a planning meeting of a cooperative education team is the actual production of a cooperative lesson, which should be represented in some type of lesson-plan format such as that presented at the end of this chapter. The "minutes of outcomes" section of the worksheet is intended to ensure the equitable distribution of other tasks that should be accomplished in preparation for teaching the lesson. Periodic review of minutes and lesson plans may help in monitoring equity in work distribution. If such monitoring reveals that one or two team members regularly assume the majority of tasks, it is a sign of problems with positive interdependence. Team members may be "freeloading," taking advantage of the group's size to avoid work. Some members' interest may be waning. Those doing most of the work may not trust others to carry out assignments. Inequity in the division of labor is an enemy of a team's sense of cohesion and requires the team to explore its causes and possible actions to re-establish balance (e.g., limiting the number of responsibilities for which a single person may volunteer).

We offer two final bits of advice regarding the planning of a cooperative lesson. First, plan together, face-to-face; do not attempt to separately design lesson components and then "jigsaw" them together. Jigsaw planning inevitably results in duplications, omissions, and a less efficient, effective, enjoyable cooperative experience for both students and teachers alike. Face-to-face interaction is as important for collaborating adults as it is for collaborating students. Second, take time to identify problem situations that may arise (e.g., absent students, behavior challenges of individual students, confusion regarding complex directions, attempts to compete rather than cooperate) and, more importantly, to detail approaches upon which all team members can agree for preventing problem situations from occurring or for intervening in such a way that teacher disruption of group work is minimized.

Conducting Cooperative Learning Lessons

When conducting a formal lesson, one critical role of the cooperative education team is to clearly explain to students the *task, the goal structure(s), and the social skills being stressed,* that is, whether it is a cooperative, individualistic, and/or a competitive learning structure. Another is to monitor the effectiveness of the cooperative learning groups and to intervene to provide assistance with the task (e.g., answer questions, clarify or teach parts of the task) or to improve students' interpersonal and group skills. Two final roles of team members are to evaluate students' achievements and to discuss with students how well they collaborated with each other.

Conducting a formal cooperative learning lesson requires the cooperative education team's joint adherence to its lesson plan. A lesson should be more than the delivery of instruction; it is also a time to collect data on several levels and to make adjustments that improve the present and future lessons. During the lesson, designated members of the team provide students with a clear explanation of the academic content, the social skills, and the cooperative activities in which they are to engage. Team members monitor not only the effectiveness of the student learning groups, but also their own effectiveness in coordinating actions to deliver the lesson as designed or to adjust the objectives, activities, or performance criteria during the lesson if student responses signal this need. Of course, making on-the-spot changes in the lesson requires that the team have a plan for making adjustments. At a minimum, this plan should identify who makes which adjustment decisions as well as how and when the decisionmakers will confer during the lesson and communicate the changes to the other participating team members.

During a cooperative group lesson, members of the cooperative education team are responsible for intervening to assist students with task or interpersonal problems, and to evaluate and review with students their academic and social skill performance. They are also responsible for intervening to assist one another in performing their agreed-upon roles in the lesson (e.g., providing prompts to a team member who forgets or makes an error with an important direction, action, or piece of information). The review of their own performance evaluations may occur briefly at the end of the lesson and, most certainly, at the team's next planning meeting.

Teaching cooperative lessons on a frequent and regular basis has many benefits. Team members have the opportunity to observe colleagues' demonstrations of new or exemplary instructional approaches and to learn from their colleagues' models. The members also have the opportunity to be observed by trusted colleagues who are also acquiring knowledge and competence in using cooperative learning in the classroom. Peer-coaching models, such as that suggested by Cummings (1985), provide a structure for teammates to refine their instructional skills by receiving specific constructive feedback. Finally, frequent and regular implementation of cooperative lessons builds a teaching team's cumulative history of successes—examples of strategies that have worked in the past when addressing various challenges—as well as examples of less effective interventions, all of which helps the team to develop more-successful future lessons. The cumulative history of successes also builds team confidence and cohesion, which in turn leads to future success.

Evaluating Cooperative Learning Lessons

Evaluation continues after the lesson, with the team's further evaluation of students' performance and their own self-evaluation. One of the first items on the agenda of any planning meeting that follows a cooperative lesson should be an evaluation of the team's performance—of the integrity of the lesson's delivery, the effectiveness of instruction, the team's ability to coordinate their actions and work together, and the teams acquisition or refinement of skills through the teaming process. Evaluation results inform the team of how future lessons can be better designed and conducted.

Table 2 offers a series of evaluation questions that cooperative education teams may wish to address in meetings. Of course, all the questions rely on observational data collected when the lesson was delivered. Questions that deal with the behavior of team members also require a high level of trust among teammates and skills in giving and receiving positive and negative feedback (Johnson & Johnson, 1991).

Self-reflection, self-evaluation, reviewing successes and failures with others, and evaluation of others' (students' and teachers') performances are all evaluative actions that promote professional growth among members of the cooperative education team, as well as improving cooperative learning experiences for students. When members of cooperative education teams are evaluating performance and providing feedback to one another, it is especially important for them to remember to structure reward interdependence, that is, shared rewards and celebrations for the team's collective work. Reward interdependence means that the recognition of one member's contributions does not overshadow the possibly less visible, but equally important, contributions of another. A

Table 2. Sample evaluation questions for cooperative learning teaching teams

Integrity of Cooperative Group Learning Lesson Delivery

To what extent was the lesson delivered as designed? Did team members perform their designated roles? What could be done to improve members' role performance?

Did adjustments need to be made? Why? What was learned from making the adjustments?

To what extent were the critical elements of face-to-face interaction, positive interdependence, individual accountability, and social skill development and processing structured into the lesson?

To what extent was attention to academic and social skill objectives balanced?

To what extent did team members successfully anticipate problem areas and employ effective interventions? What are likely future problems and appropriate interventions?

Use of Effective Instructional Methods

Were the academic and social skill objectives appropriate for the learners? What are appropriate objectives for the next lesson? How did/will team members provide additional guided practice or enrichment for those who need it?

Do certain individuals or groups of students require individualized objectives, materials, or performance criteria in the future? If so, what will be done to individualize and measure student success?

Did team members respond to students in a consistent manner?

Was the explanation of the objectives, process, and expected outcomes clear? How might it be improved in subsequent lessons?

How did the team check for students' understanding of the content and the cooperative group task? What are alternative ways of checking for understanding in future lessons?

Modeling of Collaboration

How did the team members provide a model of effective collaboration for their students? How might the team provide an even more effective model of collaboration in future lessons?

Did team members fulfill their agreed-upon roles and responsibilities in the design, implementation, and evaluation of the lesson? What is each team member most proud of in designing, implementing, and evaluating the lesson?

Do team members feel that they equitably distributed responsibility for instructing, monitoring, and evaluating the performance of all of the students in the class?

Skill Acquisition

What did each team member learn from watching their colleagues teach?

Do team members want to set individual professional growth objectives for

(continued)

Table 2. (*continued*)

the next lesson? How do team members want their colleagues to help them monitor their progress?

Team Membership
Does the team need additional expertise? What sources of training, modeling, coaching, and feedback are available?
Is it time for the team to expand or dissolve? If so, why?

---

norm within effective collaborative education teams is that successes are celebrated collectively—no one person receives special recognition. As a result, when goals are achieved, all members share in the gratification of having contributed to the achievement. One responsibility of cooperative education teams and of the administrators that support their work is to jointly explore and identify what it is that team members view as a reward or an incentive for continued collaboration. At a minimum, teams should structure celebration time into every meeting's agenda. During this time, each member shares at least one positive statement about cooperative lesson–related activities, the students, or other professional accomplishments.

It must be remembered that along with joint rewards comes joint responsibility. There will be times when a lesson goes poorly, when a student presents an exceptional challenge, or when things, in general, do not work out as hoped. Teams that swim together must also sink together; when a team faces disappointments or failures, it is the collective "we," and not an individual, who accepts responsibility.

CASE STUDIES: EXEMPLIFYING
TEACHER ROLES AND DECISIONS

Below are three examples of cooperative education teams in action. Each is a composite of the actual experiences of a number of cooperative education teams functioning in Vermont schools. The descriptions are intended to illustrate the diversity among teams in terms of their composition, size, and the way in which they handle the critical elements of cooperative learning structures.

1. An Elementary School Language Arts Team

In a school committed to providing children with heterogeneous learning environments, a 15-year veteran teacher of the 4th grade and a novice special educator new to the school system collaborate to meet the needs of all of the students in a 4th-grade classroom. Fourth graders who are eligible for special education or other special services receive their support within this general education classroom.

The two teachers differ tremendously in training background and experiences. In the past, the 4th-grade teacher relied primarily on a basal series to teach her students to read; the special educator was trained to deliver instruction in phonics to individuals or small groups of learners. One similarity between them was a mutual interest in cooperative learning. The 4th-grade teacher had recently completed a course in cooperative learning, and the special educator had had experience with cooperative groups in his graduate training program. This team decided to use cooperative learning groups in two areas of reading: 1) drill and practice in sound–symbol relationships and 2) answering comprehension questions about passages in the basal reading text. They met a minimum of twice a week to plan lessons, and they co-instructed every day during the 45-minute reading block.

From the start, the two teachers shared responsibility for selecting objectives and materials. Every lesson included a review of phonetic skills and a set of comprehension questions for student groups to answer. During the first marking period, the 4th-grade teacher assumed primary responsibility for the lesson design. She presented the task to the students, while the special educator assisted in monitoring student progress in social skill acquisition. The classroom teacher collected anecdotal data for four student groups; the special educator collected data for three groups. Both teachers provided students with feedback on their use of collaborative skills. The classroom teacher graded all the papers and provided feedback on academic performance to the students and their parents.

During the second marking period, the special educator took on a more active role and co-designed lessons with the classroom teacher. On occasion, he also explained the task and social skill objectives to the students. By the third marking period, the classroom teacher and the special educator were rotating roles and responsibilities on a daily basis. One explained the objectives, task, and expected outcomes, while the other assumed primary responsibility for monitoring and evaluating individual and group performance of the desired social skills. They also took equal responsibility for grading student assignments, meeting with parents during parent–teacher conferences, and providing one another with feedback on their instructional skills.

Both teachers found this partnership stimulating and professionally valuable. In an effort to further refine their skills and better meet student needs, they decided to expand the membership of their cooperative education team. They invited a Chapter 1 teacher, who had expertise in alternative strategies for teaching reading and in the development of thematic units, to team teach with them and attend their Tuesday and Thursday planning meetings. The original two-member team believed the Chapter 1 teacher could help them to develop interdisciplinary units, motivate the students, and breathe new life into the team. The Chapter 1 teacher accepted because she wanted to learn cooperative group instructional methodology so that she could meet the needs of her students within the classroom, rather than through a "pull-out" service delivery model. She also welcomed the opportunity to develop a closer professional relationship with her colleagues. Two years later, in 1992, all three instructors continue to meet twice weekly for planning and to team up to deliver language arts instruction a minimum of 4 days a week.

2. A Middle School Social Studies Team

A 6th-grade social studies teacher and a special educator have worked as a cooperative education team for 4 years. They team teach a minimum of 3 days a week. This team does not have a set meeting time for planning. Instead, they mutually decide, from week to week, when and where they will conduct the next planning meeting. Neither team member has had formal training in cooperative group learning, but both have had the opportunity to team teach extensively with other school personnel who are considered outstanding in the design and delivery of cooperative group learning experiences. In addition, both team members have had training in effective instruction and collaborative teaming (Thousand & Villa, 1992). They try to employ the principles of collaborative teaming when they meet to plan cooperative learning lessons.

This team has chosen to split academic- and social-instructional responsibilities. Because of his knowledge of social studies content and his enthusiasm for the subject matter, the classroom teacher determines and explains the academic objectives. The special educator, who is familiar with various social skills curricula and is experienced in facilitating social skills groups for middle-level students, determines and explains the social skill objectives. Both teachers monitor student progress and intervene to teach academic and social skills. The classroom teacher makes sure that students summarize their learning daily, while the special educator guides the evaluation of whether collaborative skill objectives were met.

The members of this team also decided to take a summer graduate course in cooperative learning together and to invite colleagues with more experience and expertise in cooperative group learning to observe their classes at least once each marking period and provide them with feedback.

3. A Secondary School Science Team

A high school science teacher who had formerly relied primarily on whole-group instruction and lab activities to teach homogeneous groups of high-ability students decided to try cooperative learning structures.

She gave two reasons for taking this new instructional approach. First, she had received strong written negative feedback from her department chair about her continued failure to use a variety of instructional approaches. Second, the school board had adopted a policy that virtually eliminated homogeneous grouping and tracking from the high school. The teacher recognized that soon the composition of her classes would be more diverse and that new instructional strategies, such as cooperative group learning, might enable her to better meet her students' needs and please her supervisors.

During the previous year, the science teacher had overheard several teachers in the lounge commenting on how a special educator (referred to as a collaborating teacher in this school system) with expertise in speech and language had assisted them in acquiring or refining their cooperative learning instructional skills. In addition, the science teacher thought that this collaborating teacher had a great sense of humor and might be an enjoyable work partner. The science teacher approached the collaborating teacher with an invitation to form a cooperative education team for the class period prior to lunch; the invitation was quickly accepted. The collaborating teacher saw it as an opportunity to acquire content knowledge that would assist him in working with students who were eligible for speech and language services and who were struggling with the vocabulary and content of the science classes.

The science teacher (with her expertise in the specific subject matter) and the collaborating teacher (with his expertise in cooperative learning, verbal and nonverbal communication, effective instruction, and techniques for individualizing and adapting instruction) formed a cooperative education team in 1990. During the first year, they discovered numerous differences in their educational philosophies and their approaches to teaching and classroom management. Initially, the collaborating teacher reported feeling more like a teaching assistant than a teacher during the actual instructional period. In retrospect, he identified the primary source of those feelings as his lack of content mastery during the first year of the team relationship. The science teacher noted that she felt very dependent on the collaborating teacher for the design and presentation of the cooperative learning segments of lessons. She also stated that were it not for the skill and patience of the collaborating teacher, she would have given up using cooperative learning structures.

The science teacher readily acknowledged the many skills she had acquired in order to design more active student-learning experiences and to accommodate student differences. The collaborating teacher pointed to the science content he had acquired and the skills in conflict resolution that were refined as he and his teammate developed a classroom-management system that was mutually acceptable. Interestingly, both acknowledged that discipline problems diminished as the students were trained in how to work as members of a cooperative learning group and given more responsibility for their own and one another's acquisition of academic and social skills.

During the second year of the team relationship, a student with Down syndrome enrolled in the team's "college-level" biology course. She provided the team with the opportunity to refine skills in designing group-learning experiences in which student objectives are individualized. The team wanted this learner to both contribute meaningfully to group activities and achieve her individualized education program (IEP) objectives. They decided on several strategies. First, a peer tutor, a former student who had demonstrated mastery in the science content of this class, was recruited by the science teacher to pre-teach some of the science content to the young woman during her study hall. The collaborating teacher provided initial and ongoing training, support, and evaluative feedback to the peer tutor. Second, they frequently assigned the student with Down syndrome the role of timekeeper in her group, thus addressing the time-telling and timekeeping needs identified in her IEP. Third, they reduced the amount of content for which this student was held accountable. Fourth, with the permission of the young woman and her parents, the members of her cooperative group assisted her and her teachers in determining appropriate instructional and social skill objectives, accommodations, and modifications.

The members of this cooperative education team express confidence in their ability to design exciting and appropriate group-learning experiences. Both are involved in planning for the transition of a young man with multiple disabilities to their school. The science teacher has requested that this young man be placed in one of her classes and, with her collaborating teacher teammate, has begun designing cooperative group science lessons to address his IEP goals of increased vocalization, communication-board use, and age-appropriate social interactions, along with the academic and social skills of the other students in the science class.

CONCLUDING COMMENTS

We have described how classroom teachers and support personnel can effectively share expertise and responsibility for designing, conducting, and evaluating cooperative learning experiences, and thus personalize curriculum and instruction for students who, by nature, have unique and changing needs. As the case studies illustrate, teaching need not be a "lonely profession" (Sarason, Levine, Godenberg, Cherlin, & Bennet, 1966, p. 74), and the traditional pull-out and special-class arrangements of compensatory and special education need not be the solution to the challenges of increasing adult-to-student ratios, individualizing instruction, and accommodating student differences. When members of the school community work together to foster the academic and collaborative skill development of students, they offer the students a valuable model of collaboration in action, as well as providing opportunities for their own professional and interpersonal growth.

It is important to remember that it may take a cooperative education team some time to become as effective and efficient as its members would like for it to be. Teams evolve throughout the forming, functioning, formulating, and fermenting stages of group development, particularly if their members regularly examine the role clarification questions in Table 1 and the evaluation questions in Table 2, and if they review how well they use small-group social skills. Numerous teams also report that the agenda format presented in the team meeting worksheet is most helpful in alerting them to the crucial elements of an effective team (i.e., frequent face-to-face interaction, positive interdependence, individual accountability, social skill performance, periodic assessment, of instructional and interpersonal effectiveness).

The task of educating an increasingly diverse student population can be overwhelming. No one teacher is capable of successfully meeting this challenge alone. We propose that collaboration among students (through cooperative learning structures) and adults (through cooperative education teams) is a key to meeting the challenge of educating a heterogeneous student population, and are pleased to report that students themselves have also joined adults as partners in cooperative education teams and have proven to be creative participants in formulating objectives, instructional methods, and accommodations for individual students (Villa & Thousand, 1992). When the work of the traditional teacher is divided between two or more persons, both teachers and students can more fully experience the power of being able to meet increasingly diverse educational and psychological student needs, free themselves from isolation and sole responsibility for student learning, and experience the fun and feeling of belonging that result when people reinvent education together.

REFERENCES

Brandt, R. (1987). On cooperation in schools: A conversation with David and Roger Johnson. *Educational Leadership, 45*(3), 14–19.

Cummings, C. (1985). *Peering in on peers.* Edmonds, WA: Snohomish.

Glasser, W. (1986). *Control theory in the classroom.* New York: Harper and Row.

Glickman, C.D. (1990). *Supervision of instruction: A developmental approach* (2nd ed.). Boston: Allyn and Bacon.

Harris, T. (1987, October). *A speech and language pathologist's perspective on teaming to accomplish cooperation between and among regular and special educators for the provision of services in the least restrictive environment.* Paper presented at Vermont's Least Restrictive Environment Conference, Burlington.

Johnson, D.W., & Johnson, R.T. (1987). *A meta-analysis of cooperative, competitive and individualistic goal structures.* Hillsdale, NJ: Lawrence Erlbaum Associates.

Johnson, D.W., & Johnson, R.T. (1991). *Learning together and alone: Cooperation, competition, and individualization* (3rd ed.). Englewood Cliffs, NJ: Prentice Hall.

Johnson, D.W., Johnson, R.T., Holubec, E., & Roy, P. (1984). *Circles of learning.* Arlington, VA: Association for Supervision and Curriculum Development.

Parnes, S. (1981). *The magic of your mind.* Buffalo, NY: Creative Education Foundation Inc., in association with Bearly Limited.

Parnes, S. (1988). *Visionizing: State-of-the-art process for encouraging innovative excellence.* East Aurora, NY: D.O.K. Publishers.

Sarason, S., Levine, M., Godenberg, I., Cherlin, D., & Bennet, E. (1966). *Psychology in community settings: clinical, educational, vocational, and social aspects.* New York: John Wiley & Sons.

Showers, B., Joyce, B., & Bennett, B. (1987). Synthesis of research on staff development: A framework for future study and a state-of-the-art analysis. *Educational Leadership, 45*(3), 77–87.

Skrtic, T. (1991). Behind special education: *A critical analysis of professional culture and school organization.* Denver, CO: Love.

Slavin, R.E. (1984). Review of cooperative learning research. *Review of Educational Research, 50,* 315–342.

Slavin, R.E. (1987). Ability grouping and student achievement in elementary school: A best-evidence synthesis. *Review of Educational Research, 57,* 293–336.

Slavin, R.E. (1989). Research on cooperative learning: Consensus and controversy. *Educational Leadership, 47*(4), 52–54.

Smith, S.C. (1987). The collaborative school takes shape. *Educational Leadership, 45*(3), 4–6.

Thousand, J.S., & Villa, R.A. (1990). Sharing expertise and responsibilities through teaching teams. In W. Stainback and S. Stainback (Eds.), *Support networks for inclusive schooling: Interdependent integrated education* (pp. 151–166). Baltimore: Paul H. Brookes Publishing Co.

Thousand, J., & Villa, R. (1992). Collaborative teams: A powerful tool in school restructuring. In R.A. Villa, J.S. Thousand, W. Stainback, & S. Stainback (Eds.). *Restructuring for caring and effective education: An administrative guide to creating heterogeneous schools* (pp. 73–108). Baltimore: Paul H. Brookes Publishing Co.

Villa, R.A., & Thousand, J.S. (1992). Student collaboration: An essential for curriculum delivery in the 21st century. In S. Stainback & W. Stainback (Eds.). *Curriculum considerations in inclusive classrooms: Facilitating learning for all students* (pp. 117–142). Baltimore: Paul H. Brookes Publishing Co.

COOPERATIVE GROUP LESSON PLAN

Lesson name: _____   Authors: _____

What is the content area? _____

What are the appropriate age levels for this lesson? _____

I. ACADEMIC OBJECTIVES

1. What are the prerequisite skills for taking part in the lesson?

2. What are the academic objectives of this lesson? (*Remember to also identify the social skills objectives in Section IV.*)

3. What, if any, are the modifications of objectives for students with special needs?

II. FACE-TO-FACE INTERACTION DECISIONS

1. Group size (2–6)?

2. Which students will be in which groups? (Assignments should ensure that students are heterogeneously mixed.)

3. How is the room arranged? (Draw a diagram.)

III. STRUCTURING POSITIVE INTERDEPENDENCE

(Members should get the messages: "We sink or swim together," "Do your work—we're counting on you," "How can I help you to do _____ better?")

1. How will you structure one group goal? A single product? A shared outcome?

(continued)

COOPERATIVE GROUP LESSON PLAN *(continued)*

2. Will you structure a group reward (e.g., a single grade for all group members, dual grades for individual and group products, dual grades for academic and social skill performance, bonus points if pre-set criteria are exceeded, free time or privileges for meeting criteria)?

3. What student roles will be used to promote positive interdependence? (Define each role, using the words that you will use with the students.)

4. Will there be any division of labor other than assigning roles? Describe.

5. How will materials be arranged to promote positive interdependence (e.g., one set of materials, "jigsawing" of information or materials)?

6. How else will positive interdependence be structured? (optional)

   (a) Will you structure intergroup (between group) cooperation? How?

   (b) Will you structure intergroup (between group) competition in order to develop within-group cohesion? How?

   (c) Will you structure positive fantasy or identity interdependence? How (e.g., a fantasy mission, selecting a group name)?

IV. ESTABLISHING SOCIAL SKILL PERFORMANCE

1. What are the social skills for this lesson?

(continued)

83

COOPERATIVE GROUP LESSON PLAN (continued)

2. How will the need for each social skill be communicated? Who will do this? (e.g., After groups have worked for a few sessions, ask them to brainstorm the behaviors needed to help the group learn and work together well; tell students why the skill[s] is/are important; ask students why the skill[s] is/are important.)

3. How will each social skill be explained? Who will do this? (e.g., Someone demonstrates the skill, explains each step of skill performance, and redemonstrates the skill; someone structures a role play of the skill for the whole class, explains each step of skill performance, and structures a second role play of the skill; a videotape is used to demonstrate and explain the skill.)

4. How will the social skill[s] be assigned to group members? (e.g., Assign the skill[s] generally to the groups, so that all group members are responsible for engaging in the social skill[s]; assign the skill[s] to randomly selected students, and rotate the skills around the group until all members have performed each skill several times; select target students who need coaching and special training and pre-train them in the skills.)

V. SOCIAL SKILL PERFORMANCE: TEACHER MONITORING AND INTERVENTION

1. How will the groups be observed? Who will observe which groups? (e.g., Anecdotal observations and notes are made regarding specific examples of students demonstrating cooperative behaviors; a structured observation form is used, and each group is observed for an equal amount of time; a structured observation form is used, and only selected groups that are having trouble are observed.)

2. How will teachers give students feedback if the target social skills are being used? (e.g., Interrupt the group and compliment them on the use of the skill; during review, compliment the group on the use of the skill; say nothing.)

3. How will teachers give students feedback if the target social skills are not being used? (e.g., Ask the members of the group what they have done so far to increase the use of the skills; ask the group what they will try next to increase skill use; suggest an action.)

(continued)

COOPERATIVE GROUP LESSON PLAN *(continued)*

4. What are some likely problems in collaboration? What are some interventions that might help avoid/remedy them? (Rules: When you feel like intervening, don't. If you must intervene, do it with a question, not an answer. Move away as soon as you can, even if it is only 3 feet.)

VI. SOCIAL SKILL PERFORMANCE: STUDENT MONITORING

1. Will there be student observers?

2. What social skills will the student observers monitor?

3. Will the students observe one or more groups?

4. Will the students observe for the whole lesson?

5. How will the student observers be selected?

6. How and when will student observers be trained? Who will train them?

7. How and when will student observers share their observations with group members?

VII. STRUCTURING INDIVIDUAL ACCOUNTABILITY

How do teachers determine whether each student learned the material and contributed to the group effort and product? (e.g., roam among groups and randomly question individuals, individually quiz all students, select only one paper to represent the group.)

(continued)

COOPERATIVE GROUP LESSON PLAN *(continued)*

VIII. SETTING THE TASK

1. How will the academic task and criterion for success be explained? Who will explain them?

2. How will the social skill(s) and criterion for success be explained? Who will explain them? (Always tell the students what the objectives are, give or solicit from the students reasons why it is important to learn this content or perform this task, be specific in your directions, and check for students' understanding.)

IX. AFTER THE LESSON: CLOSURE AND REVIEW

1. Closure: Following the lesson, how will students summarize what they have learned? (e.g., Teachers randomly ask questions of individual students, the entire class gives a choral response or signal, students do a quick "5-minute write" in response to questions.)

2. How and when will students receive feedback on their academic performance? Who will assess which students, and who will provide the feedback?

3. How will teachers' observations be shared? (As a general rule, share negative comments in private and positive comments in both public and private.)

4. In addition to hearing observation reports from teacher and peer observers, how will students assess their individual and group success in using social skills?

From Villa, R.A., & Thousand, J.S. (1993). Redefining the role of the special educator and other support personnel. In J.W. Putnam (Ed.), *Cooperative learning and strategies for inclusion: Celebrating diversity in the classroom* (pp. 57–91). Baltimore: Paul H. Brookes Publishing Co.

TEAM MEETING WORKSHEET

ATTENDANCE

Persons present
(Note late arrivals)

Absentees

Others who need to know

ROLES

Timekeeper:
Recorder:
Equalizer:
Others:

This meeting

Next meeting

AGENDA

Items

1. Positive comments
2.
3.

Time limit

5 minutes

4.

5. Evaluating (task & relationship) 5 minutes

6.

7.

8.

9. Evaluating (task & relationship) 5 minutes

MINUTES OF OUTCOMES

Action items Person(s) responsible

1. Communicate outcomes to absent members and others who need to know by: (date)_____

2.

3.

4.

5.

AGENDA BUILDING FOR NEXT MEETING

Date: Time: Location:

Expected agenda items:

1.

2.

3.

4.

The reader has permission to photocopy this form for educational purposes.
From Villa, R.A., & Thousand, J.S. (1993). Redefining the role of the special educator and other support personnel. In J.W. Putnam (Ed.), *Cooperative learning and strategies for inclusion: Celebrating diversity in the classroom* (pp. 57–91). Baltimore: Paul H. Brookes Publishing Co.

5

Cooperative Classroom Management
Student Needs and Fairness in the Regular Classroom

LUANNA H. MEYER
AND LEAH A. HENRY

The strategies presented in this chapter and the experiences on which they are based arose from a collaborative public school–university partnership, the Syracuse Stay In School Partnership Project, designed to better meet the instructional and sociopersonal needs of middle school students regarded as being "at risk" because of their attendance records and academic performance. The program was not a pull-out or traditional remedial effort to address these needs; instead, the participants attempted to work together to change the school and classroom experiences of young people who were, for various

Portions of this chapter were adapted from Meyer (1992). Classroom strategies described in this report were developed as part of the Syracuse Stay In School Partnership Project, which was funded by the New York State Education Department, in a collaborative effort with the Syracuse City Middle Schools, Syracuse, New York. The opinions expressed herein do not necessarily reflect the position or policy of the New York State Education Department, however, and no official endorsement should be inferred.

We wish to thank the participating administrators and teachers from the Syracuse City School District for their many contributions to this work. In addition, the first author would like to acknowledge the support of the Department of Special Education at the University of Washington, Seattle, during the preparation of this manuscript while on sabbatical leave as a visiting scholar.

reasons, not engaged in active participation and learning. Throughout the project, teachers have emphasized developing their own skills in order to accommodate diverse learning styles and encourage mutual student support through techniques such as cooperative learning and multicultural education. Beginning in fall 1991, these efforts focused on creating communities of teachers and students (smaller subgroups of students and their teams of teachers within the larger school population) at each of four city middle schools, and were eventually expanded to support thematic instruction and interdisciplinary teaching across teams of general and special educators. What we attempt to describe in this chapter is how such efforts at building community through explicit organizational, instructional, and peer-collaboration structures can result in the emergence of a new, positive social unit—a classroom that is fair (Evans, 1991). We believe that fair classrooms provide a context of shared understandings between teachers and students—*all* students—that allows cooperative classroom management to replace the more traditional external-contingency disciplinary methods typically used in today's schools.

Throughout the chapter, we include student perceptions, their own descriptions and interpretations of events. As part of the evaluation of a district program to reduce the occurrence of at-risk status, selected students were interviewed at different times during the school year, including both those who were regarded as being at risk based on attendance and academic performance and those who were doing well in school. The reader will find that these students' words can be harsh; many of those quoted here have a long history of negative interactions in schools. Students can be both our best and worst critics. When their words ring true and clear, they point out the same kinds of "theoretical" and "empirical" problems that educators write about in the professional literature, and these complaints must be heard. We believe that it is *particularly* important to hear these voices when their descriptions and interpretations make us uncomfortable. School is the place where children spend the majority of their waking hours, where they become socialized into their culture and community, and where they develop and refine their interactional patterns with others—with both peers and those in authority. The way that children themselves perceive the environment that we have created for them is critical; without knowing students' own viewpoints, we cannot be certain that our best intentions have indeed resulted in the kinds of processes and outcomes that we planned.

UNDERLYING ASSUMPTIONS

We make several assumptions in presenting these experiences and ideas. First, whether a teacher is certified in general education, special education, or as a specialist (e.g., in reading, or in English as a second language), or has some combination of possible licensures, the typical classroom served by that teacher comprises 15–30 young people with a variety of abilities, needs, and interests, but all of whom are usually within 1–2 years of one another's chronological age (although by the secondary level, the age range can be somewhat greater). That is, teachers in America teach in age-graded classrooms—a "model" that has remained virtually unchanged for over 50 years. As a consequence, many specialized instructional techniques designed to address the needs of individual children don't fit easily into the typical class structure, which makes one adult responsible for rather large groups of children for various periods of a typical school day. How exactly, for example, does one find time for a private consultation with one middle school student? What "behavior management" plans for one student's problems will blend readily into a 3rd-grade classroom?

Second, educators do not "hand pick" the children in their classrooms, nor should they. As teachers, it is our job to do our professional best to address the needs of whichever children find their way into the classroom each year, without exception. (Where there are serious mismatches between teacher and child, the teacher—as the person in power—must protect the more vulnerable child by ensuring that whatever changes are made are truly in the best interest of the child, and not made for the benefit of an adult who refuses to accept the natural challenges of teaching.) Every classroom will include some children who will learn no matter what, who will reinforce the teacher's every teaching behavior, and every classroom will also include children who do poorly time after time, children who resist the teacher's efforts to teach, and children whom educators struggle to understand, and sometimes manage to reach with extraordinary teaching. The experts tell us that these children bring out the best in us, because, unlike the self-starters, these are the children who need us the most and whose growth is in direct measure a function of our accomplishments as teachers. But as teachers, we all know that taking on these challenges is a risky business: it's great when we succeed, but we feel terrible when we fail. Perhaps one of the reasons that teachers sometimes seek to place children out of their classrooms is to avoid the possibility of failure.

Third, children come to school with a host of memories and experiences. Despite our myth of each new school year as a "clean slate," children bring complex histories with them to school, and the older they get, the more likely it is that they will view school and their teachers with distrust, anxiety, and suspicion. For too many children, school is not a place that makes them feel safe or secure or proud of themselves. For example, one student in our program whom we shall call Susan was experiencing her first year in a large urban school system that was regarded as progressive. Her new school was obviously very different from those that she had attended in another state, schools in which corporal punishment was used as a disciplinary technique. Yet she saw similarities rather than differences in the ways that the schools treated students:

> Susan: I like this school better [than my old school]. At least they don't hit you and make you stand in the corner like a fool. But I'm not sure what is worse, a hit or the embarrassment that goes on here. The teachers be yelling at you in front of the whole class and tellin' everyone your business. . . .
> Interviewer: Do you think the teachers discipline for a reason?
> Susan: Yea, they have a reason, to make you look stupid and embarrass you, just like in [my old school]. But I don't start no trouble, cause like I told you, I learned my lesson.

For perhaps most children, school is a place where their personal fears and worries are translated into objective and public embarrassments —school can mean poor grades, failures, peer rejection, alienation, and building strong walls out of "I-don't-care" attitudes to protect oneself from feelings of inadequacy. School programs and policies such as special education and retention for academic failure are ostensibly designed to support student mastery, but they can also negatively affect self-esteem and create conditions leading to peer rejection. Richard, for example, had been receiving resource-room support for his learning disability, had been retained twice, and, despite the fact that he was passing his courses at the time of the interview, had this to say about school:

> It's going to be the same as always. I'm here to learn. I'm not repeating another year. I'm not spending another year in this place. . . . I'm tired of people calling me stupid and making fun of me. . . . They gave me a rough time last year, they give me a rough time this year, so next year when I go to high school no one is going to say a thing to me. . . . It just doesn't seem fair that I have to be separated from my friends. Everybody else is in high school now and I'm here.

A single teacher cannot change a child's self-concept overnight, but must instead expect change for the better to progress slowly, as part of a long-term struggle with the negative memories that led to low self-esteem in the first place. Furthermore, improvements must be maintained from year to year: one good year or one good teacher can easily be forgotten when followed by failures for the child.

The assumptions behind this chapter are based on the reailities of today's classrooms and today's children, within the context of a society that needs to do far more to support education and children's learning than is now being done with our limited budgets, outdated age-graded classroom models, and crowded, poorly equipped schools. Our expectation is not that classroom teachers can magically solve every behavioral and emotional problem that comes their way. In fact, one purpose of this chapter will be to encourage teachers to access the community resources that should be available to support students in the general classroom and outside of school (including, for example, mental health services for families). Another recommendation is that teachers fully expect the school and district administration to provide the academic and behavioral support needed by teachers and students, and that some "school coping strategies" be developed. But the major challenge of this chapter is to look at classroom management in a different way by viewing the class as a community of cooperation. To achieve this, our major goal must be to create a community of support in the classroom, to provide an environment in which children can feel psychologically secure. Nothing beneficial can follow unless students first believe that schools and classrooms are safe and fair places.

FAIRNESS AND THE CULTURE OF THE SCHOOL

Schools and classrooms are primarily seen as environments in which to deliver the academic content that children will need in order to succeed in society, but they are also social systems. Indeed, everyone will acknowledge that both teaching and learning are difficult, if not impossible, if the classroom climate is not conducive to these tasks. This implies an orderly classroom in which children receive support for mastery without disruptions that might interfere with their academic work.

In the process of creating educational environments in which learning is possible, schools model a social order for children—for most children, the first social system that they experience outside of the family. It is therefore logical to expect that children will learn not only academic content in school, but also something about the nature of social systems and, to the extent that a school is a microcosm of a society and reflects it values, about the nature of the society in which they live. In America, schools are charged with the dual responsibility of achieving both excellence and equity, and we expect our public school system to provide an "equal opportunity" for children to achieve to the best of their ability. But what do schools actually teach children about the social structure of American society?

Inequality in School

In his discussion of the need to be more explicit and careful in teaching children about important ideals and values, Berman (1990) writes: "We teach reading, writing, and math by doing them, but we teach democracy by lecture" (p. 2). We *tell* children about ideals such as democractic participation and equal educational opportunity, but whether or not schools actually model those ideals is open to challenge. Eric, for example, typically attends school no more than 2–3 days each week, and is described by his 7th-grade teachers as being "unmotivated" and a "troublemaker." As one teacher put it, "It's a shame, that kid is going to drop out before he ever reaches 10th grade." Yet Eric was one of the first students named by the teachers on his team when selecting the top 10 math students to represent the school on a state test. One teacher challenged Eric's lack of participation:

> *Teacher:* Eric, if you don't make decisions about your own well-being and the situation you confront, then you are only giving up having control over your life. If you continue to give up control by ignoring people and not making decisions, then you are basically saying that you do not want to control what happens to you. Do you want other people controlling your life? No! You need to make a choice, so that you can have control.
> *Eric:* Listen, I don't want to be here, and I really do not care what group I am in. . . . You can decide.

When Eric continued to refuse to play an active role, he was sent to in-school suspension. In one sequence of events, Eric was truant for 3 days in a row, on Monday, Tuesday, and Wednesday. When he appeared in school on Thursday, he was given a 3-day in-school suspension. Eric attended the in-school program for 2 days, then told the interviewer: "This is ridiculous, I'm not spending another day in in-school. I'm not coming on Monday." After missing Monday, he was given another 2 days of in-school suspension, bringing his total of missed school days to 8—which then resulted in failing grades in five of his classes. How did Eric interpret these events? In his words:

> *Eric:* I learned if you don't do your homework, you get suspended. I learned if you don't do what the teacher says, you get in trouble. But it's always like that. Either you do what they say, or they throw you in the in-school [suspension program]. I just wish someone would have listened to why I didn't do my work. I mean, it's not like I couldn't do it. It only took me a half hour to make up all my missed work, and the rest of the day I just sat there. . . . I don't care though! In-school is boring, but it is better than being picked on by the teachers. . . . I just want some respect.
> *Interviewer:* Has school taught you about respect?
> *Eric:* Yeah, that I'm not respected. . . . I always thought respect was something you give if you wanted it back. I see other kids talking back to teachers and fighting, and they get more respect than I do. That's unfair. I thought respect was letting other people talk when it is their turn, and having the same done for you. No! It's like they jump at every chance to punish you, whether or not they hear your side of the story.

Do students like Eric have a distorted view of the school climate? Eric suggests that teachers treat him differently than they do certain other students; despite their statements about self-determination, Eric seemed to believe that the teachers were not really interested in his point of view, but merely wanted him to comply. Ellen Brantlinger (1991) recently published a fascinating account of the perspectives of teenage students on their own and others' transgressions and the resultant disciplinary consequences. She studied two distinct groups—high-income and low-income adolescents. There were remarkable differences in the reported perceptions of how these two groups of students were treated in the same schools by the same teachers. The low-income youths experienced a greater number and variety of disciplinary penalties that were described as being disproportionate to the "crime" and humiliating in nature. Although most of the transgressions committed by the high-income youths were described as being playful pranks, virtually *anything* that these young people did was far more likely to be simply "laughed off" by school authorities. These discrepancies were, incidentally, reported by *both* groups of teenagers: school was consistently seen as being more unfair for the low-income children.

We have noticed a similar double standard operating in schools, although the division that we studied was not along family-income lines, but instead seems to show discrimination against students based on personality. The student who could be described as articulate, witty, and extroverted in a personable way seems more likely to have his or her behavior "laughed off," even though his or her actions are violations of well-known and generally enforced rules. The student who is withdrawn and quiet, who might be described as less sociable, or in some cases antisocial, would be quickly punished for breaking a rule. We have already heard from Eric, who is socially isolated from his peers and only speaks when spoken to; the following is an actual event that Eric experienced. Drew, in contrast to Eric, is an extrovert who would be described as popular by both peers and teachers alike. Ironically, Drew displays many of the disruptive behaviors that school rules were designed to modify, including talking in class, talking out of turn, and swearing in the halls.

At the school that Drew and Eric attend, no student is permitted to enter a classroom after the bell has rung for the start of the period. If a student is late for class, a note that includes an explanation for his or her tardiness must be obtained from the main office.

One Monday, Drew, a "high personality" student, entered the class 10 minutes late. He made his entrance in a loud manner, interrupting silent reading time. The teacher said, "Drew, where were you? You're late!" Drew replied, "Chillin' and maxin' with my homeboys. Look, Teach, I lost track of time, then lost my notebook." The teacher smiled, put her arm around Drew's shoulder and said, "What am I going to do with you? If you don't have a silent reading book, get one from the bookshelf. You only have five minutes left in silent reading."

The next day, Tuesday, Eric, a "low personality" student, arrived at the classroom door just as the teacher was closing it. Eric was looking down at his feet as he attempted to walk past the teacher. The teacher said, "Eric, you realize you are late, and I have no choice but to send you to the office. You know the rules." Eric began to say something in what was described as a mumble, "But I couldn't find my notebook, and Ms. B. stopped me in the hall." The teacher replied, "Listen, we have rules in this school for a reason, and if you don't follow them, suffer the consequences. Goodbye, and don't come back without an admittance slip."

Another example of the double standard was observed during a class outing to a local historic site. During lunch time, at a cluster of picnic tables outside, the teachers informed the students that no food was to be thrown. One student—a boy whom we would characterize as "high personality"—was caught in the act of throwing food, and was given two verbal reprimands: "Stop doing that, I'm watching you," and, "Eat your lunch, don't throw it." Another student, who might be described as "low personality," was also seen throwing food and was told: "Hey, what do you think you're doing, mister? You're lucky you got to go on this trip at all. Now pick up that food, and the next time I have to say one word, you're on the bus and in in-school [suspension] tomorrow."

When some of the students were asked about any differences in the way that rules were enforced, they had this to say:

Beth: If the teachers like you, you get away with murder. And if they don't well, you're in for it. . . . I don't really have any problems because the teachers like me, but kids like Eric and Joe, the teachers think they are troublemakers, and so they get treated like it.
Richard: I remember last year, I'm in class working. Other kids were running around me fighting and junk. They yelled at the teachers and talked back. They passed, they never got in trouble, but they never seemed to do any work. It doesn't seem fair when some people interrupt. The teacher says nothing. And the minute you do one thing, the teacher freaks out. . . . It's like if a group of you will be doing something, you get in trouble and the other kids run off smiling.
Joe: I learned the hard way, no matter what I do I get busted.
Eric: I'm basically screwed. Whether I commit the crime, chances are I'll do the time. So I just say nothing. And anyway it's not like anyone is going to listen. I'm screwed if I do and screwed if I don't. What's the difference?

When asked whether he thought this was unfair, John replied: "They already have their mind made up. What can I do? You can't change [it], so lets talk about something else." Eric just walked away.

In his book *Savage Inequalities*, Jonathan Kozol (1991) examines disproportionate funding that allows schools in wealthy neighborhoods to spend as much as three to four times per pupil as those in low-income neighborhoods. He discusses this subject with a group of well-to-do teenagers and asks them what they think about the situation. When asked directly if they would be in favor of a more even distribution of resources for schools that would enable poor kids to get a better deal, the students' replies are disturbing. With only one or two exceptions, the wealthy kids responded that they did not see how that would benefit them—no, they said, let's keep things as they are. Kozol asks why the attitudes of America's elite are so seldom studied by researchers: what are the implications for democracy in America if these reported attitudes are widely representative of what different groups of children think?

What Are the Consequences of Unfair Schools?

Berman (1990) argues that a school culture that sacrifices the teaching of social responsibility and positive interdependence in the quest for academic excellence and competitiveness may ultimately fail to produce a democratic citizenry. Imagine the consequences of a hierarchical school system wherein the elite receive more opportunities and have a positive school experience, and all other students continue to attend school year after year primarily to round out the normal curve and attain "minimal competencies." The most alienated of those young people—some say as many as 25% of today's 9th graders—will refuse to participate in this demeaning situation, leaving school as soon as they reach the legal age. Many of these "drop outs," as they will be known, will have few employment skills, little motivation to seek out further opportunities to better their circumstances through education and training, and may even be angry, bitter, and willing to lash out at a system that they feel has treated them poorly throughout their lives. Will the composite product of our present educational system provide a strong foundation for the democratic ideals of this nation?

Berman (1990) challenges the dominant "ideology" of child development that most teachers in European–American culture learn, which emphasizes Erikson's goals of autonomy, individuation, and independence as the most valued signs of the fully developed adult (Erikson, 1968). Gilligan (1982) argues that this description of the developmental process is not accurate; for example, she reinterprets the adolescent's struggle for autonomy not as a struggle to separate from others but as an attempt to renegotiate relationships with others such that the subservient role of the child would be replaced by one of equality and influence. "The adolescent desires connection, affiliation, and involvement, but wants to experience his or her own power, authority, and influence within that connection" (Berman, 1990, p. 9). Interestingly, educators practicing multicultural education have drawn on different cultural perspectives to place a similar emphasis on the value of interdependence in children's development into socially responsible adults. Native American cultures may not value the achievement of the individual as something separate from the social good of the group; thus, an emphasis in school on individual accomplishment and competition immediately places many Native American children in direct conflict with the mores of their culture

(Swisher, 1990). Friesen and Wieler (1988) also discuss similar issues in their analysis of multicultural education, peace education, and cooperative learning as three examples of educational movements that are actually firmly grounded in the progressive education tradition and seem well matched to our longstanding public school commitment in America.

It is possible that some of the goals presently articulated for America's schools may be used to maintain the inequities that children from different socioeconomic backgrounds experience when they come to school. Children may be indirectly victimized by a school career that does not include conscious and carefully planned efforts to create equality of opportunity by providing the additional supports that may be needed for those whose resources outside of the school setting are minimal or even grossly inadequate. An emphasis on academic excellence and "world-class standards" can be interpreted by a school as a mission to identify and create a group of students who are the "best in the world" in various subject areas: in such schools, competition and individual achievement are most important to students, teachers, parents, and the school board. Often, even a focus on values in school emphasizes individual well-being over that of the social unit, with the ideal being a school system that supports personal choice and individual responsibility. In fact, for many people, the dominant national values of our country may very well be seen as independence and self-reliance, rather than mutual support and cooperation.

Can Teachers Teach Children About Fairness?

Teachers working in schools can do little on a day-to-day basis about the inequitable distribution of school funds and resources among different schools (although they *can* become effective advocates for a more equal distribution of resources). Teachers can, however, determine whether or not the students in their schools experience a classroom culture that is fair to them or one that mirrors the same kinds of injustices that Brantlinger's interviewees reported (1991). The process of creating a culture of fairness in the school begins with an examination of our goals for students and of the instructional strategies used to reach those goals. Teachers who are committed to creating a school culture that is fair to children, one that makes children—all children—feel valued, can begin by critically analyzing the instructional structures of their classrooms by answering questions such as these:

How do you teach? Are your students exposed to many different opportunities to learn, or only a few, such as large group lecture and independent seat work? In any given week, do your students experience more than a few of the following learning opportunities: lecture, experimentation, discovery learning, computer-assisted instruction, one-to-one remedial assistance, peer tutoring, cooperative learning groups, seatwork, homework, discussions with one another and with resource people?

How many "new" educational approaches have you mastered in the last 3 years? Have you used, for example, natural ("whole") language approaches to math and reading, cooperative learning, reciprocal teaching, interdisciplinary or thematic teaching, portfolio assessments, journals, or peer support networks?

Have you incorporated relevant multicultural pedagogy and curricular content in your subject area into your teaching and your students' learning?

In your classroom, do your student-evaluation procedures require some students to do less well in order to distinguish those students who do "better"? Do your goal structures encourage students to separate themselves from one another, or are they equally respectful of both individual and group accomplishments? Are students encouraged to support one another's learning and personal growth, or are they encouraged to compete with one another?

Before you leave these questions, go back and read them once again from the perspective of a student who has been a challenge for you. How would that student answer each question? The bottom line, of course, is whether students think that the culture of their school is fair for others and for themselves. What do you think your students would say if questioned on this point?

THE SYRACUSE STAY IN SCHOOL PARTNERSHIP PROJECT

Our own work in Syracuse at the middle school level might best be characterized as a collaboration among school and university personnel to support innovations that are incorporated into the basic structures of the school and the general education classroom. Some of these efforts are focused on creating instructional dynamics within the classroom that take advantage of the potential for positive peer interrelationships and students' support of one another's learning, rather than viewing groups as something to be "managed." Thus, both cooperative learning and interdisciplinary teaching are critical components of this model. As MacIver and Epstein (1991) note:

> Many proponents of the middle-school philosophy view the establishment of interdisciplinary teams of teachers as the keystone of education in the middle grades (e.g., Merenbloom, 1986; Vars, 1987). They hypothesize that interdisciplinary teams will eliminate the isolation that many teachers feel by providing a working group of colleagues to conduct activities and discuss and solve mu-

tual problems; that instruction will be more effective in schools that use inter-disciplinary teaming because of increased integration and coordination across subjects; and that teachers on a team sharing the same group of students will be able to respond more quickly, personally, and consistently to the needs of individual students. (pp. 596–597)

Thus, in addition to a focus on interdisciplinary teaching, interdisciplinary teaming activities help professionals to create collegial support networks among teachers and school support staff.

Interdisciplinary Teaming

Structure   Our project activities supported 7th-grade interdisciplinary teams that included from six to seven teachers (in the content areas of mathematics, science/health, English, reading, social studies, and special education) at each of four middle schools that had made a 2-year commitment to each group of approximately 135 7th graders. Each group of students was basically a random sample of the 7th graders enrolled at each school (each building had a total of two to three teams at each grade level) including students both with and without disabilities, those in general education and those who were receiving special services. Team planning and interdisciplinary teaching provided teachers with mutual challenges and supports to explore innovations such as cooperative learning, multicultural education, continuous progress evaluation (enabling all students to graduate from 7th to 8th grade while allowing them 2 years to achieve 8th grade competencies, rather than retaining some for a second year of 7th grade), and a new program to integrate perspectives on academic skills and career awareness.

Building Community   A major purpose of the teams was to break down the usual impersonal middle school population patterns whereby 12- and 13-year-olds generally go from one 40-minute period to another in different configurations of 25–30 drawn from a population of hundreds of children, which differ dramatically from elementary school patterns, whereby students remain in a smaller cohesive group that stays together with one teacher throughout the school day. As a group, our 7th graders told us that they preferred elementary school and saw it as a culture that valued them more as individuals and supported them more effectively as learners. They even indicated that they wished they could return:

> Joe: I liked having just one classroom. I hate moving around. When I first started here I was so confused, and nobody helped me. I really did not know what I was supposed to do, or where I was supposed to go. . . . In elementary school, you get better help. Sometimes, I don't get things right away. In elementary school, the teacher would sit down and explain things. Here in middle school, you are on your own. The teacher always tells me

the answer is in the book. Well, how am I supposed to find the answer when I don't even understand the book?

Susan: I hate the way middle school is set up. You're in this classroom this period, the bell rings, you run to your lockers, and you're in another classroom. By the time I get to my next class, I worry so much about getting the right notebook, homework, and all that stuff, that I've forgotten what I learned the period before. In elementary school, all the stuff was in one place. There was one teacher, and more time to learn. The hardest thing is trying to remember to get to places on time, and remember the right things to bring, because if you don't you get yelled at and embarrassed. . . . I really don't like having seven teachers. . . . It's like at the end of the day, all the stuff you learned got lost in the shuffle. In elementary school, everything went together, and you really got to learn.

Beth: Elementary school was great. You were in one classroom. Everybody was friends. Here there are so many people, and you move around so much. I'm with Joe first period, and that's all. I never get to see Eric. In elementary school there were fewer people and less teachers.

Beth: I got the sense in elementary school that the teachers really cared about me. They really knew me. But now nobody really gets to know you.

Richard: I will say that elementary school was easier. Like in math I have three pages due tomorrow, stuff due in English, reading, social studies, science. It's a lot. By the time I wake up every morning, go to school, come home, do my work, eat my dinner, its time to go to bed. At least when I was little I had a life.

Yet the students did seem to appreciate that middle school was somehow preparing them for the realities of life as they grew older:

Richard: I like middle school. In a way, it's better to have a lot of teachers. Moving from class to class and remembering stuff is hard. But I think that is teaching us a lesson . . . to be responsible. After a while you get used to it. If you think about it, having a bunch of teachers teaches you about life. You learn how to deal with people. I mean, think about it, when we are out of school we will have to deal with hundreds of people, not just one.

How then can middle school accomplish its apparent purpose of bridging the more protected status of elementary school and the teen years? One student made an observation about her own feelings that may provide the answer:

Beth: What I really miss is having like a family. You know, it was nice to have the same people everyday. I knew what to expect, and everybody was friends. . . . They still teased you, but at least then they knew who you were.

Students seem to express their need to have a more stable social network in school—a sense of community within a manageable social unit of individuals who know one another well and support each other. The intention of our program's team structure is to provide this smaller network and mutual support for both teachers and children. Students become part of a subgroup of perhaps 135 children who will stay together with the same group of teachers for a 2-year period.

Team Support for Students   Weekly team meetings allow teachers to share their insights and problemsolve together to meet individual student needs. A team of teachers who share a team of students can test out one another's perceptions and develop hypotheses about situations such as the possible volatility of certain combinations of young people in a single class, lesson scheduling for a student who clearly does better with "tough" material in either the morning or afternoon, and other issues of group dynamics that emerge in different class periods attended by different configurations of students during each teacher's day. Our teams have frequently solved classroom "management" difficulties by simply changing certain students' schedules at natural breaks in the school year; there is no "rejection" of individual students implied by these decisions (the same students always remain within the group) and no single teacher is put in the impossible position of planning and implementing changes and providing supports in isolation from colleagues and the administration. It is important to emphasize that at these weekly interdisciplinary team meetings, students are not viewed as the separate responsibility of either the regular or special education teacher: each student is a team concern, and teachers pool their resources and ideas on behalf of every student on the team. In some instances, the expertise of the special education staff is used to explore certain options for a typically developing student, and in others, a particular regular education teacher may be the one to develop a significant teacher–student relationship with a student receiving special education services.

The team also provided several types of support to bridge the gap between students' lives at school and at home. Individual teachers made an effort to really get to know their students through opportunities such as eating lunch with them, chatting with them in the halls between classes, and exploring personal interests during daily advisor–advisee time. Information was brought to team meetings when it seemed important; for example, one teacher noted: "I was talking to Billy today, and I just want you all to be aware that his mother is in rehab again. As a result, he was moved in with his aunt. He really is going through a fragile and trying time . . . so keep an eye on him." Team members discussed students who seemed to be having difficulty; made phone calls and asked the school counselor or vice principal to follow-up when necessary; offered a variety of supports to students and families, both in and outside of the classroom; and would not hesitate to make a home visit if it seemed necessary or had the potential to be helpful. Much of this was done on the teachers' own time—during lunch or after school, for example. These kinds of involvements in children's lives can ensure that students do not feel ignored and alone, and can be critical in addressing serious personal needs that might otherwise go unnoticed until a crisis has developed or the student has literally disappeared from school.

At one school, the extent of the team's involvement in students' home lives was demonstrated by frequent parent–teacher team conferences. In a typical week, the team met with at least four parents to discuss issues that varied from helping different students to prepare for a major test or develop better study skills to informing parents about improvements in behavior or discussing possible causes or solutions when a student seemed to be having difficulties in school. One project that the teachers believed was particularly successful was a homework call-in affiliated with a local television station. The team would collect the list of each day's homework assignments from all teachers and call that information in to the station; parents could then call the station and simply access a recording to find out all of their child's assignments for the day, as well as learn about upcoming projects or tests and other important school events.

Team Development   Teaming is not a smooth process, however, as most teachers have never received formal preparation to work with other adults, as opposed to teaching children (see especially Chapter 4 in this volume). Thus, we also find it helpful to adopt certain structures for team meetings, including having a formal agenda, an assigned facilitator for each meeting, and a written minutes format whereby a recorder lists the agenda item, the decision made by the group, the teachers who will be responsible for each task, and the timelines for follow-up. The presence of school support staff at these meetings is also important; regular attendance by a representative from the principal's office provides both practical and moral administrative support for a group of teachers willing to do something innovative. It also makes possible the immediate resolution of any ambiguities about what is allowable (in cases in which meetings might otherwise end with "Well, we can't do that because . . . " or "Let's ask the principal and then bring it up again next week") and provides access to additional supports that are available or can be requested by the administration from the district or other sources, such as community mental health agencies or school–business partnerships. This administrative involvement is appreciated by the teachers and may also serve as a signal to other school personnel that the administration views such innovative efforts by teachers in a positive way and will provide tangible support for them. Depending on the agenda for a particular team meeting, relevant school guidance staff or even community social workers or professionals from the mental health network may attend.

Finally, the Syracuse program included on each team a faculty member from the School of Education at Syracuse University who attended these meetings and served as a resource person, helping to keep the group focused, assisting with follow-up on behalf of individual students, and even serving as mediator for some interpersonal conflicts that arose. While not all public schools have access to faculty from institutions of higher education, many could develop such relationships; we also believe that the university's teacher-education and research activities benefit from this ongoing, intimate contact with schools, teachers, and students.

Peer Support Networks

The Syracuse Stay in School Partnership Project was originally funded as an effort to prevent school drop out by improving the mainstream educational experience for students at the middle school level. We know that we have had a positive impact on many students through the implementation of various instructional innovations, including multicultural-education adaptations and cooperative learning (see Meyer, Williams, Harootunian, & Steinberg, in press, for a more comprehensive overview of our activities and the results to date). Yet, after the first 2 years of participation by approximately 25 teachers who had developed considerable personal and professional expertise in these innovations, reality has set in with the realization that mainstream reform cannot affect students who are so alienated that they do not come to school or simply refuse to participate when they do. By 7th grade, there is already a small but clearly identifiable percentage of young people with alarmingly consistent patterns of truancy, while others are so isolated from other students and teachers that they have developed extremely successful strategies to avoid all classroom and instructional participation even on those days when they do attend class. We firmly believe that nonschool agencies such as the community mental health service network must become part of collaborative efforts to serve children and families whose needs are far more complex than even severe school alienation. But even within the school environment, we determined that something more could and had to be done by teachers to encourage and structure student participation in classroom activities.

We had practice in using cooperative learning strategies, and followed the general guidelines provided in the literature on the subject in forming our cooperative learning groups. But we also believed that we could do more to take advantage of the idea of a cooperative learning "base group" that would provide peer support and serve as a source of potential friends for students who were either very socially isolated or whose only friends were clearly not a positive influence on their learning and social development. Thus, we established a process of forming cooperative learning groups to encourage the development of peer support networks around each student who had been identified as being at risk. Much has been written about the positive effects of cooperative learning on children's achievement and personal—social development. We believe that cooperative learning also provides the teacher and children in the classroom with learning opportunities that take full advantage of the human resources available to support each child within that environment. Classrooms *are* groups of children—it is much more realistic and natural to recognize the exchange of mutual support, explicit expectations for social behavior, and importance of group achievements as well as individual progress as accurate reflections of what adult society will demand of future citizens.

It is important to emphasize that although our process for creating peer support groups allowed the teachers to identify "at-risk" students, this label was not visible to the children themselves; all students were organized into heterogeneous groupings that were similar in design. This is critical to our program philosophy, as we had determined that our efforts at drop-out prevention were to involve neither pulling students out for separate treatment nor labeling or identifying them in any way. We feel that while the student who is likely to drop out might be self-identified in many ways by high school age, middle school was too early to contribute to any labeling process that might actually do more harm than good by stigmatizing students and creating possibly counter-productive clusters of students who would actually be negative models for one another if they were grouped together for so-called remedial activities. We also considered the shift to interdisciplinary teams as giving us an even better opportunity to consistently support students across the school day and throughout the marking period, as students could now be grouped with some overlap of their peer support networks across classes, and as the same model was being used by all teachers on any given team.

There are various guidelines for forming cooperative learning groups—many of these, along with useful adaptations for students with diverse needs, are discussed in other chapters in this volume. The established guidelines, however, primarily address strategies to ensure that the small, cooperative learning groups within the classroom are heterogeneous. We wanted our groups to be heterogeneous in gender, race, culture, ability, and achievement levels within a particular subject area. Yet, we also wanted to work more directly with the teachers to ensure that each student's cooperative learning group could function as a peer support network for students regarded as being at risk. Thus, we used various predictors to identify those students as early as possible (within the first month of school), and project staff met with the team at each school to deliberately structure a cooperative learning group that might potentially function as a peer support network around each at-risk student.

Identifying At-Risk Students   Our is not a perfect system, but we have developed a process to identify students who seem most in need of peer support. First, over a period of several years, we have partially validated the *School Self-Rating*, which is now moderately predictive of students who will later fail some of the classes required to move on to the next grade. The entire survey consists of 30 questions, and provides sub-scale scores for the three dimensions of academic self-appraisal, attitude toward school, and cooperation (Meyer, Harootunian, & Williams, 1991). Figure 1 shows the 13 items of the scale that we have found to be most predictive of students who will later experience difficulty in school. Again, this method is not perfect, but by using a cut-off of less than 50 points total for the 13 items, we can identify 60% of the students who (based on the previous year's actual school performance) are likely to fail their grade and/or display high rates of school absence. The survey can be administered to students as a group in their classes by the 3rd week of school; this time lag is necessary to ensure that the survey is measuring some exposure to the present year's school experience, and not simply testing memories of last year's. Scoring should take no more than a day or two, after which time the list of students scoring below 50 should be reviewed by the team. The team may elect to delete certain students whom the teachers believe are "false positives" (e.g., very good students who are almost never absent, but whose scores are right at the cut-off point); teachers in the Syracuse project have chosen to delete a very few such names at each of the schools. More importantly, however, the team spends one to two of their planning meetings reviewing the list and adding teacher referrals of names of students believed to be at risk academically and socially.

Using this process, our teams have identified approximately 20% of the students as being at risk, a proportion that is almost equal to those in previous years, which were based on actual academic achievement and attendance patterns at the end of the first marking period. We realize that this process is undoubtedly flawed, but it does give our teacher teams a vehicle for structuring direct peer-support efforts on behalf of the students whom they regard as being most in need, and it does so very early in the school year. Furthermore, as *all* students are ultimately part of these peer support networks, other students who might also be at risk, even though they were not explicitly identified by the process, are nevertheless also included in the peer support model.

The following is an example of a student who was not identified by our system, nor by our teachers, as being at risk, and yet still has certain difficulties in school that, it could be argued, are the direct result of the competitive structure of traditional classrooms. Toby's teachers described her as follows: "Oh, Toby, if I had a class full of Tobys this job would be a dream;" "Toby is a dream, the perfect student, an example for all to follow;" "Toby is bright and insightful, she is what every teacher wants a hundred of;" and "Toby is a star, a teacher's gem!" Toby actively participates in class discussions, receives perfect marks on her assignments, and is involved in many extracurricular activities, including drama and chorus. When completed assignments are returned to students, teachers

Directions

The purpose of this School Self-Rating is to find out how middle school students feel about school and about their own performance in school.

For each of the questions, you are asked to select one of several answers that best matches how you would rate yourself on that particular item. There are no "right" or "wrong" answers. Instead, it is important to give your opinion. Please be honest about your feelings!

Your answers on this survey are confidential, and only your teachers will know how you responded. Your answers will be used to help plan school activities and will not be a part of any grading procedure.

Remember, for each question, circle one answer that corresponds to how you feel about that question.

THANK YOU FOR YOUR HELP!

Answer these questions first (please print):

Name: _____

School: _____

Class: _____

Teacher: _____

Date: _____

For each question below, **circle** the letter of the answer that best matches how you feel:

1. How do you rate yourself academically compared with those in your class at school?
   a. I am among the best
   b. I am above average
   c. I am average
   d. I am below average
   e. I am among the poorest

2. How important to you are the grades you get in school?
   a. Very important
   b. Important
   c. Sometimes important
   d. Not particularly important
   e. Doesn't matter to me at all

3. Forget for a moment how teachers grade your work. In your own opinion, how good do you think your work is?
   a. My work is excellent
   b. My work is good

(continued)

Figure 1.   The predictor subscale of the Syracuse school self-rating, 1991 version.

Figure 1. (continued)

    c. My work is average
    d. My work is below average
    e. My work is much below average

4. Where do you think you will rank when you finish middle school?
    a. Among the top students
    b. Among average
    c. Average
    d. Below average
    e. Among the lowest

5. How do you think your teachers would rate your effort in school?
    a. They would think I always try my best
    b. They would think I usually try hard
    c. They would think that sometimes I try hard and sometimes I don't
    d. They would think that I usually don't work very hard
    e. They would think I don't try at all

6. Which statement best describes your close friends?
    a. All of them do poorly in school
    b. Most of them are below average students
    c. Most are average
    d. Most are above average
    e. They are probably among the best students in school

7. How hard do you try to improve your work in school?
    a. I always try as hard as I can
    b. I usually try to improve my work
    c. Sometimes I try, sometimes I don't
    d. I don't try very hard to improve my work
    e. I rarely try to work in school

8. Do you think you have the ability to finish high school?
    a. Yes, definitely
    b. Yes, probably
    c. Not sure either way
    d. Probably not
    e. No, definitely not

9. How do you think your parents would rate your effort in school?
    a. They would think I always try my best
    b. They would think I usually try hard
    c. They would think that sometimes I try hard and sometimes I don't
    d. They would think I usually don't work very hard
    e. They would think I don't try at all

10. Which statement best describes you?
    a. It's important to me to do well in all of my subjects
    b. It's important to me to pass all of my subjects
    c. I expect to pass most of my subjects
    d. As long as I pass a few courses, I'm satisfied
    e. I don't care if I pass my courses or not

11. How do you think your teachers would rate your ability in school?
    a. They would think my ability is very high
    b. They would think my ability is above average

(continued)

Figure 1. *(continued)*

    c.   They would think my ability is average
    d.   They would consider my ability to be below average
    e.   They would consider my ability to be very below average

12. What kind of grades do you think you are capable of getting?
    a.   Mostly 90 s
    b.   Mostly 80 s
    c.   Mostly 70 s
    d.   Mostly 60 s
    e.   Mostly 50 s

13. If you wanted help in a class at school, would you go to your teacher?
    a.   Yes, definitely
    b.   Yes, probably
    c.   Not sure
    d.   Probably not
    e.   No, never

Scoring Procedures

Item 6 should be scored as follows:
    a = 1   b = 2   c = 3   d = 4   e = 5

Items 1–5 and 7–13 should be scored as follows:
    a = 5   b = 4   c = 3   d = 2   e = 1

By adding these scores for items 1–13, use a cutoff of less than a total of 50 points as predictive of at-risk status. This is not a perfect system! This cutoff score predicted 60% of the students who would be determined to be at-risk according to actual academic performance at the end of the marking period. Each team should begin with the list of students generated by using scores less than 50, but should supplement the list by teacher referrals of additional students believed to be at-risk academically and socially.

---

regularly point out to the class that Toby received an A and can help if anyone has any questions. With tears in her eyes, Toby told the interviewer:

> "I'm afraid of being different. It's not my fault I'm smart. I can't help getting good grades. . . . I guess I'm just upset because the kids were saying stuff like brainiac, and teachers' pet."

In another interview, she stated:

> I have to look good. I want my hair to look perfect . . . I want people to like me.
> *Interviewer:* What makes you think you are not liked or accepted?
> *Toby:* Everybody thinks I'm so smart, and because of that I'm a nerd, so it's important that I look cool. . . . I have friends, but all the cool people don't talk to me unless they need help.

At the awards assembly, on the last day of school, Toby received the following awards:

Outstanding/highest average in math, social studies, physical education, reading, French, science, English

Highest overall average (she received a plaque and a $20 gift certificate for the local mall)

Perfect attendance award

Outstanding participation award in chorus (for both fall and spring terms)

Presidential Physical Fitness Award

During and after the awards assembly, the following statements by other students were overheard:

"Man, what's the point, when she gets all the awards?"

"Every year there's one person who ruins it for everyone else."

"That's not fair, I do well too."

"Don't you hate people like her? She thinks she is all that and more."

Do the kinds of reward structures described above motivate children? Or do children succeed despite such structures? A grandmother at a parent–teacher conference provided us with her observation: "At this age, these kids are so scared of being different. They don't want to be too smart, too short, too developed. They just want to fit in, and sometimes that's hard." How can schools support children's learning and motivation to achieve without disrupting the social networks that they are only beginning to develop?

Constructing Networks The literature on at-risk students suggests that many of these young people have poor peer relationships and that if they do have friends, they tend to be the kinds of friends who are seen as having a negative influence on their school achievement and motivation (see Evans & Matthews, 1992). Our interest in designing positive peer networks also evolves from evidence from research on peer rejection that indicates that: 1) rejection by one's peer group can contribute to making school an aversive experience for adolescents and thus motivate them to leave school prior to graduation, 2) positive social support can buffer a child against the development of various behavior and personality disorders that might otherwise emerge, and 3) a child who is already vulnerable to some disorder is further stressed if his or her negative peer relationships are not altered for the better (Garmezy, Masten, & Tellegen, 1984; Kupersmidt, Coie, & Dodge, 1990). Our own interviews with teachers suggest that many of the middle school students who are seen as being most at risk are socially isolated and, in certain cases, might well be labeled as clinically depressed. These students have virtually no school behavior—they are often absent, and when they do attend school, they keep to themselves and do not participate in classroom interactions with other students. A few of them are characterized by aggressive, acting-out behavior and friendships with peers who are similarly acting-out, thus fitting the pattern described by Evans and Matthews (1992).

Interestingly, there is no empirical data base on the design of positive peer supports for students at risk. To compensate for the absence of any real guidance in the research literature, we have drawn on our own backgrounds and clinical experiences in structuring student–peer interactions, inclusive schooling for students with disabilities, and special education for students with emotional disturbance (Meyer & Putnam, 1988). Our criteria for constructing the peer-support networks were, therefore, necessarily clinical and experiential. We begin constructing the networks by having teachers participate in a general training session on the subject. An experienced teacher provides a scripted example with information on the different characteristics of individual students from a typical class; each teacher team then uses this sample class for practice in constructing peer support groups for one instructional period. The necessary information about individual students is collected prior to forming the groups by asking students to provide information about themselves on individual index cards, including their name, age, grade, gender, race, favorite activities outside school, and content-specific preferences. For example, in English class, the student is asked to indicate what he or she regards as a strength or interest related to English. Once this information has been gathered by each teacher, the team is ready to construct a focus peer-support network, or cooperative learning group, for each student.

For logistical reasons, the team selects one class period when all of the students are attending classes (with no pull out), and are approximately evenly distributed across the teachers. The teacher who has a particular at-risk student during that class period focuses on establishing a peer support network for him or her, which the remaining team members will also seek to maintain to some extent throughout the marking period. All team members participate in the discussion about each at-risk student's peer support network, working through every teacher's focus class period until everyone on the team has developed an initial roster. Following this team process, the teachers share their networks with one another, and each teacher is then generally able to work on an individual basis to construct his or her cooperative learning groups for the remaining class periods.

We have found teachers to be quite knowledgeable after just a month of school regarding their students' school interests, academic achievement, and peer interaction patterns; within the team, at least one teacher is likely to have learned something about each individual student. Table 1 lists the criteria that we use to construct the peer support networks, which begin by following the general principles for forming cooperative learning groups, move on to delineate specific criteria for our peer-support–networking model, and also include specific suggestions for selecting a positive peer-group member for an at-risk student. Note that the

Table 1.   Criteria for constructing peer support networks

General Criteria for Groups

Each group in the class period should be heterogeneous with respect to:
  Gender
  Ethnicity (e.g., African American, Native American, EuroAmerican)
  Achievement levels in the subject area
  Academic ability
  Preferred in-class activities (e.g., writing versus speaking)

Specific Criteria for Peer Support Networking

With rare exceptions, no more than one "at-risk" student per group

If a student receiving English as a Second Language services is in the group, try to also include another student who is bilingual (same first language) but more fluent in English

Avoid potentially explosive or otherwise negative group combinations (e.g., two volatile students who would set one another off, a "macho" boy with "victims," too many off-task students within the group)

Try to plant one "worker" and/or a "diplomat/peace-keeper" in each of the groups

Building Specific Peer Supports

For each group, select at least one and possibly two students who might be a potential friend for the student at risk. These matches should:
  Be good influences/models
  Have similar interests/hobbies
  Be of similar academic ability (although doing better academically and/or attending school more regularly)
  Seem to be a good personality match with the at-risk child (How to judge? Use your observations/best hunches).

goal is not to identify so-called "star" students as potential friends. Instead, teachers should identify students who are very much like the student at-risk, with one important exception: this potential friend would be regarded as a positive influence because of his or her personality, positive attitudes toward school, and school performance. The potential friend does not have to be a high achiever or a popular student, but he or she should be someone who the teacher thinks has an adequate sense of self, can reach out to peers, and does work in school, and whose academic achievement is generally acceptable, rather than either excellent or poor. The students are told that they are being grouped heterogeneously, but the other criteria for formulating the groups to support positive peer relationships are not discussed with the students. We rely on time spent working together as the context for the possible development of positive friendships and peer supports within the groups.

The peer-support networks stay together for their class cooperative learning activities for at least a 10-week marking period. In some instances, the original group combinations will not work, and modifications will have to be made. During team planning meetings, teachers can share ideas about new directions when initial efforts do not go as well as expected. In most instances, this model has had a remarkable impact on children who were previously isolated from peers and who showed little sign of engagement in school instructional activities. These youths made friends, and even when their achievement in other contexts lagged behind, made significant academic progress during cooperative learning activities. Eric provides an illustration of how a change in instructional strategies can have a ripple effect on several dimensions of a student's experiences:

> As described earlier in this chapter, Eric is a student who displays few signs of engagement during classroom instruction. During the cooperative learning structure in math class, Eric's behavior and performance changed dramatically. In other classes, Eric would slump in his seat and show all the signs of disengagement—this was most pronounced when the teacher was presenting material in a traditional lecture format. In contrast, during cooperative learning group time, he voluntarily participated and actually led his group through the assignments. He became a group leader, helping those who did not understand, encouraging peers, and keeping the group on task.
>
> The change was particularly evident during shop period. For a month, Eric entered the shop class at the bell and talked to no one during the entire period. A student from the special education class was then placed in the shop class during this period, and the teacher paired him with Eric, using the buddy system to provide the exceptional student with a natural support. Eric took the student under his wing, answering questions, instructing, and guiding him through the individual projects. Once the other students had the opportunity to see how well Eric worked with his assigned buddy, they began asking him questions and for help on their projects. By the end of the 10-week marking period, Eric had become a major source of support and assistance for peers, who either voluntarily sought his assistance or were guided to him by the teacher.

The peer support networks, although originally intended to address the social and academic needs of individual students, served to alter the schooling experiences of all students. Cooperative group structures and expectations allow each individual student to experience success and positive participation in learning situations that have previously been associated with negative feelings for many of them. Teachers report that "management" needs are essentially redefined in such classroom structures: students are safe in their base groups, and previous opportunities for friction between students and misunderstandings between students and the teacher have been restructured. But in some cases, important needs remain unmet. In the final section, we suggest some possible directions for meeting those needs.

ADDITIONAL SERVICES AND SUPPORTS FOR STUDENTS IN NEED

Berman (1990) emphasizes the importance of developing a sense of "community" among students in school through which they become socially conscious and thus capable of intervening to improve the ability of the group to live and work together. He defines community as follows:

> A community is a group of people who acknowledge their interconnectedness, have a sense of common purpose, respect their differences, share in group decision-making as well as in responsibility for the actions of the group, and support each other's growth. Classrooms and schools can be these kinds of communities, but it takes time, intention, and new forms of shared leadership. (Berman, 1990, p. 11)

Of course, Berman is talking about sharing leadership with students, charging them with the responsibility of defining the group's values, and then asking:

> What guidelines could we establish for ourselves that would not only make this a productive class but would also make this a safe place for people to share what they are thinking and feeling, and a safe place for people to make mistakes and learn from them? (1990, p. 11)

Berman goes on to stress the importance of having students also be involved in evaluating whether the group is functioning well, and being able to address and resolve conflicts that may arise. The important point is that once again in this case a traditional assumption about "classroom management" based on the teacher as the controlling agent in the school environment would no longer apply. The use of cooperative learning over time should "instruct" students in the necessary group-evaluation and social skills that they will need in order to participate meaningfully in addressing conflicts that may arise within the classroom and in different school situations. Indeed, the structure of peer support networks is intended to create an even more intensive and individually tailored "community" around the needs of children while also giving them an even safer subgroup in which to acquire and practice academic, social, and group-evaluation skills.

Yet, teachers may be successful in creating school-as-community classrooms and still find that the individual needs of some students seem to be beyond the community's ability to help. Our schools have been expected to do far too much with far too little. Many of today's students arrive at school with their basic emotional and physical needs unmet. Their families may be living in poverty and/or may be somehow dysfunctional for the child, so that the resources and structure necessary for learning prosocial behavior and empathy for others simply may not be available outside of the school environment. If teachers do share regular planning and problemsolving sessions with other team members and school support personnel, the intensive needs of children who continue to be a challenge are far more likely to receive a "full hearing" and all of the benefits that the school has to offer. But this may still not be enough.

Teachers have a right to expect two additional supports, and we must become effective advocates to make these expectations clear to our school administration and home communities. First, our traditional models of school suspension and expulsion make little sense as reactions to actions by children and youth who clearly sometimes provoke such consequences on purpose. Perhaps such techniques were never really intended to help children, but were instead designed as strategies to remove "troublemakers" from the classroom and the school. Where will these young people ultimately go? The long-term consequences for a society that has reacted to negative behavior by helping to force the student away from the one environment that might provide a structure for learning new behavior could be devastating. Rather than postponing the problem until a suspended or expelled child becomes an antisocial adult with no marketable skills, schools must develop new disciplinary procedures that do not rely on isolating students from the school and learning environments. Some of our schools have established quite successful "in school" suspension procedures whereby children never leave the building but do receive more intensive supervision from support staff, while still being expected to complete their work regardless of behavior.

Ian Evans suggested several years ago that perhaps the time has come for schools to instruct children in how to react in a behavioral emergency (Evans, 1988). It is interesting that we continue to have fire and storm drills in schools and expect our citizenry to learn techniques such as the Heimlich maneuver, CPR, and mouth-to-mouth resuscitation, yet still allow them to remain ignorant of how to react to events such as seizures and behavioral outbursts. In today's world, it might be extremely useful for people to learn how to react safely and reasonably when a dangerous situation develops. We would recommend that every school building convene a task force or charge their pupil-services team with developing guidelines for both an in-school suspension system and a behavioral emergency drill to prepare for the possible extremes that might occur, rather than risking random panic and continuing to rely on excluding children from school or even calling the police for ordinary disciplinary situations.

Second, and most importantly, school districts must begin to develop formal interagency agreements with community mental health agencies for child and family support services that should and must be provided in addition to educational services. As noted above, a small but clearly identifiable percentage of children in school—some in special education and some who have never been labeled—show evidence of severe emotional and psychosocial support needs. They and their families may be amenable to assistance from a more normalized community mental health service, and school districts often do have access to information about those services. School may be a natural conduit for linking families and the mental health service delivery network. Particularly for children who seem headed for involvement with the criminal justice system, intensive service coordination provided in collaboration with the community mental health agency could provide a proactive starting point leading to a far better outcome for all. Each school and agency will be slightly different, but in our experience, the services do exist and are available outside of the education network. Teachers should, as a matter of course, expect their superintendent's office and state education agency to develop relevant interagency relationships and help them follow through when such services are needed.

REFERENCES

Berman, S. (1990). The real ropes course: The development of social consciousness. *ESR Journal: Educating for Social Responsibility, 1,* 1–18.

Brantlinger, E. (1991). Social class distinctions in adolescents' reports of problems and punishment in school. *Behavioral Disorders, 17,* 36–46.

Erikson, E. (1968). *Identity: Youth and crisis.* New York: Norton.

Evans, I.M. (1988, November). *Family and community supports for intervening with behavioral challenges.* Paper presented at the New Zealand Conference on Community Integration, Dunedin, New Zealand.

Evans, I.M. (1991). *Fair work, fair play: Patterns of interaction and social cognition in elementary classrooms mainstreaming students with severe handicaps.* Paper presented at the Robert Gaylord-Ross Memorial Symposium on Social Skills, Vanderbilt University, Nashville.

Evans, I.M., & Matthews, A.K. (1992). A behavioral approach to the prevention of school dropout: Conceptual and empirical strategies for children and youth. In M. Hersen, R.M. Eisler, P.M. Eisler, & P.M. Miller (Eds.), *Progress in behavior modification.* Sycamore, IL: Sycamore Press.

Friesen, J.W., & Wieler, E.E. (1988). New robes for an old order: Multicultural education, peace education, cooperative learning and progressive education. *The Journal of Educational Thought, 22,* 46–56.

Garmezy, N., Masten, A.S., & Tellegen, A. (1984). The study of stress and competence in children: A building block for developmental psychology. *Child Development, 55,* 97–111.

Gilligan, C. (1982). *In a different voice.* Cambridge: Harvard University Press.

Kozol, J. (1991). *Savage inequalities.* New York: Crown.

Kupersmidt, J.B., Coie, J.D., & Dodge, K.A. (1990). The role of poor peer relationships in the development of disorder. In S.R. Asher & J.D. Coie (Eds.), *Peer rejection in childhood* (pp. 274–305). Cambridge: Cambridge University Press.

MacIver, D.J., & Epstein, J.L. (1991). Responsive practices in the middle grades: Teacher teams, advisory groups, remedial instruction, and school transition programs. *American Journal of Education, 99,* 587–622.

Merenbloom, E.Y. (1986). *The team process in the middle school: A handbook for teachers.* Columbus, OH: National Middle School Association.

Meyer, L.H. (1992). Cooperative behavior management: Incorporating "behavioral intervention" into the design of the regular education classroom. In J. Putnam (Ed.), *Celebrating diversity.* Missoula: Montana Developmental Disabilities Council.

Meyer, L.H., Harootunian, B., & Williams, D. (1991, April). *Identifying at-risk status and preventing school dropout.* Paper presented at the Annual Meeting of the American Educational Research Association, Chicago.

Meyer, L.H., & Putnam, J. (1988). Social integration. In V.B. Van Hasselt, P.S. Strain, & M. Hersen (Eds.), *Handbook of developmental and physical disabilities* (pp. 107–133). Elmsford, NY: Pergamon.

Meyer, L.H., Williams, D.R., Harootunian, B., & Steinberg, A. (in press). An inclusion model to reduce at-risk status for middle school students. In I.M. Evans et al. (Eds.), *Perspectives on school change to prevent school drop out: The New York State Partnership experience.* Baltimore: Paul H. Brookes Publishing Co.

Swisher, K. (1990). Cooperative learning and the education of American Indian/Alaskan Native students: A review of the literature and suggestions for implementation. *Journal of American Indian Education, 29*(2), 36–43.

Vars, G.F. (1987). *Interdisciplinary teaching in the middle grades: Why and how.* Columbus, OH: National Middle School Association.

6

Supporting
Young Children's
Development Through
Cooperative Activities

JoAnne W. Putnam
and Loraine J. Spenciner

During the preschool years, children like Andy and Dawn in the following example, if given the opportunities, are able to absorb the rudimentary rules of social interaction. Indeed, if given encouragement, they are able to engage in and distinguish among three distinct types of learning and play situations: individualistic, competitive, and cooperative.

> Children at the White Bridge Preschool Center enjoy building many different types of structures in the block area. One day Dawn, a child who is developing typically, and Andy, a child with an orthopedic impairment that keeps him from walking, built a bridge out of large cardboard bricks. There were only enough bricks to build one bridge. Dawn carried the bricks

This work was supported in part by Grant #H024D0029 from the Early Education Program for Children with Disabilities, Office of Special Education and Rehabilitation, U.S. Department of Education. However, endorsement of chapter contents by the Department should not be inferred.

The authors would like to acknowledge the inspiration and support given by Richard van den Pol, Director, Division of Educational Research and Service, School of Education, University of Montana.

The order of authorship is alphabetical; the author's contributions to this chapter were equal.

from the storage shelf while Andy stacked them at the bridge site. Initially, they had disagreed about who would place the bricks, and where, but then they decided to take turns making the placements. While they coordinated their work on the bridge, they talked about how high this bridge should be and about other bridges that they had seen. After working for what they considered a long enough period, they declared the bridge finished. Then they celebrated, taking turns crawling under the bridge and congratulating each other on their achievement.

Building the bridge was a fun activity for Dawn and Andy, but it was also important in another sense: it was a cooperative learning experience. Because the task was mutually rewarding and required that they coordinate their actions, Dawn and Andy learned some important social skills—how to share, to work together, to communicate, and to compromise.

Andy and Dawn's bridge building is a good example of a cooperative learning activity. Each wanted to build a bridge, but neither had access to enough blocks. So they worked together to build one bridge. Their goals were thus positively correlated.

In some situations, cooperation prevents a no-win ending. For example, when two children have a dispute over who will get to play with a doll, an authority figure may award the doll to one child (a competitive situation—to the victor go the spoils); or take it away from both (a no-win ending); or explain how the children can share: "If you take turns being mother and (big sister or father) you can both play with the doll at the same time." The last solution is another example of a cooperative activity.

Children need to experience all three types of learning situations in early childhood programs: they need to learn how to work and play by themselves; to engage in light-hearted, rather than "dog-eat-dog," competition with one another; and most importantly because of their experience levels, to work and play cooperatively with others. All three types of learning situations can be incorporated successfully into preschool program activities.

How does one introduce cooperative activities to young children who so far have focused only on their own needs and desires? The setting is unimportant; cooperation works in a variety of early education settings, including private or public preschool and center or home-based child care. The makeup of the population is also unimportant: children with diverse abilities, including those who are developing typically and those with special needs, can successfully engage in cooperative activities. What counts in cooperative activities is what a child *does*, not what makes him or her different; as long as everyone pitches in and works together, these activities provide welcome and rewarding experiences for children as well as staff members.

In this chapter, we describe some ways to introduce and support co-operative activities in any group of preschool children. Our suggestions are practical; for example, we explain how to enhance social-skill development (a major goal of early childhood programs), and how to modify relevant activities to promote the success of children with special needs. We illustrate these goals with descriptions of cooperative learning in action in early childhood settings and conclude with an activity plan that shows how the basic elements of cooperative learning can be incorporated in a familiar format. The plan can also be modified in many different ways in order to meet specific needs. The chapter focuses primarily on children of ages 3–5, but some of the practical strategies for conducting cooperative activities pertain to children through the age of 8 and others can be adapted for use with older children.

COOPERATIVE ACTIVITIES:
WHY AREN'T THEY USED MORE WITH YOUNG CHILDREN?

Given the well-documented benefits of cooperative learning for school-age children and adults (see reviews by Johnson & Johnson, 1989; Slavin, 1990), why haven't early childhood educators employed cooperative learning strategies more extensively? Perhaps their reluctance is due to the lack of instruction on cooperative learning in college and university teacher-preparation programs, or to the lack of research or of information on this topic in the early childhood literature. Cooperative learning might also be avoided because of the prevailing beliefs that young children: 1) are unable to engage in cooperative play, and 2) may be unable to reap the benefits of cooperative learning that accrue to older children and adults. In this chapter, the authors address these and other issues that have not yet been extensively discussed in the literature.

Cooperative Play

Over the years, developmental theory has greatly influenced the philosophy of many early education programs. Early theorists (Parten, 1932; Piaget, 1951, 1959, 1968) emphasized the specific, invariant sequence in which behaviors emerge and cognition develops as children interact with the environment. These early theorists stressed the critical importance of early experiences that help a child move from one developmental stage to the next.

More than half a century ago, when the study of children was relatively new, Parten (1932) described a developmental sequence of play and emerging social interactions with peers based on her own observations. This sequence moves from unoccupied behavior, solitary play, onlooker behavior, parallel play, and associative play, to cooperative play. Her definition of cooperative play involves children sharing common goals and dividing labor. According to Parten, cooperative play develops at about 4 1/2 years of age.

In many early education programs, individualistic and adult-directed activities are emphasized: children play with materials (e.g., paints, Legos, toy cars, or blocks) or engage in activities led by adults (e.g., story time or fingerplays). Free play or unstructured activities involving pairs or groups of children take place, of course, but these are rarely specifically structured to encourage cooperative learning. However, interest in cooperative learning activities for young children is growing (see Cartwright, 1987; Foyle, Lyman, & Thies, 1991; Goffin, 1987). Cartwright (1993, p.12) aptly noted that "Cooperative learning in the classroom is not only relevant to life; it may be childhood learning at its best."

Perspective-Taking

Another reason why early childhood educators have not used cooperative learning activities is that they question whether young children are mature enough to actually profit from them. For example, one of the benefits of cooperative learning is increased perspective-taking abilities. Social perspective taking is defined as "the ability to understand how a situation appears to another person and how that person is reacting cognitively and emotionally to that situation" (Johnson & Johnson, 1989, p. 67). In the past, it was generally accepted by researchers in the fields of child development, psychology, and social psychology that preschool children were unable to engage in meaningful perspective taking. Children at the preschool level are known to be very egocentric in their thinking; they see the world from their own point of view, rather than those of others (Piaget, 1959).

However, many researchers have come to believe that, in some situations, even children from 12 to 18 months of age exhibit the ability to assume another's perspective (Borke, 1973). These abilities are fostered when children have specific opportunities to consider others' perspectives (Damon, 1983). In an early childhood setting, it is not uncommon to witness examples of children taking another's perspective—when showing a picture book to a younger peer, for example, a child will turn the book so that its pages are oriented to face the listening peer (an example of cognitive perspective-taking). Playmates are often observed comforting a distressed or crying child whose mother has just left the room (an example of emotional perspective taking or altruism). Many researchers now believe that perspective-taking abilities are fostered whenever children have opportunities to interact with others (Hill & Reed, 1990).

Lack of Research Evidence

Dr. Robert Slavin, noted expert and researcher on cooperative learning and education, states that there is currently no research base documenting the effectiveness of cooperative learning when used with preschool or kindergarten children (personal communication, January 5, 1993). Although elements of cooperative learning have been used with young children for decades (e.g., having children work or play in pairs to reach a mutual goal), studies of sustained and systematic use of cooperative learning methods have yet to appear in the literature. According to Slavin, cooperative learning is not appropriate for children who lack independent work skills or rudimentary cooperative skills. However, he notes that the literature provides some excellent examples of programs that employ elements of cooperative learning in working with young children.

Drs. David and Roger Johnson strongly advocate the use of cooperative learning in early childhood settings: "If there is anything humans are genetically predisposed to, it is to exist in consort" (R. Johnson, personal communication, January 5, 1993). However, skills needed to affiliate and cooperate are not instinctual; they must be learned. What better time to begin learning cooperative skills than in the early years? Johnson and Johnson (in press) have written a book, *Cooperative Learning for Little Ones: Let's Start Early*, that makes this point. With their colleagues, they have conducted research on 6-year-olds, finding that participation in cooperative learning groups leads to improved cognitive reasoning, among other benefits (Johnson, Skon, & Johnson, 1980)

The issue of whether cooperative learning activities are appropriate for preschool children, and in what form, has yet to be resolved by researchers. Educators need to know more about how to modify cooperative activities to make them developmentally appropriate for young children. We raise this issue as an important topic that merits greater discussion and research.

THE BENEFITS OF COOPERATIVE LEARNING FOR THE PRESCHOOL CHILD

Within the context of cooperative activities there is potential for children to learn through attending and observing; exploring and doing; coordinating, imitating, and initiating; and discussing ideas with peers. Piaget believed that when children interact and discuss matters they become less egocentric, because each of them realizes that not everyone thinks the same way that he or she does. Cognitive conflict can arise when two or more children hold different opinions on a matter. By resolving the cognitive conflict through explaining their own point of view and listening to those of others, children can be led to more developmentally advanced understanding (Tudge & Caruso, 1988).

Increasing Cognitive Development

Researchers (Murray, 1972, Perret-Clermont, 1980) have studied children's (ages 5–7) performance on conservation tasks when they worked individually and in pairs. Perret-Clermont used Piaget's classic conservation task, in which children pour liquid from two identical glasses into a short, wide glass and a tall, narrow glass. The pairs of children (a conserver and a nonconserver) were only allowed to drink the liquid (orange juice) after they agreed as to whether one child had more than the other or they both had equal amounts. The control group consisted of children (nonconservers) working individually on the same task. Then, a posttest on the conservation task was given to all the children individually. It was found that children who were paired with more advanced partners were later able to solve conservation tasks of a higher level. Studies such as these have led Piagetians such as Damon and Murray to recommend increased use of cooperative activities with young children. Moreover, these researchers recommend that teachers foster discussion and even "argument" among children about the nature of conservation (or other problems) because such interaction, in and of itself, helps children to learn and to reach correct conclusions.

Enhancing Social and Emotional Development

Social and emotional development have been recognized as important predictors of later academic success. In *Facilitating Play*, Smilansky and Shefatya (1990) discuss the relationship between sociodramatic play and outcomes such as increased language skills, higher intellectual competence, and better emotional and social adjustment. Sociodramatic play involves "pretend" circumstances and roleplaying. With some creative thinking, the variety of play themes that can be selected (i.e., "house," "school," or "going to the carnival") are unlimited.

Odom, McConnell, and McEvoy (1992) report the results of a study in which preschool special education teachers were questioned about the social competence of the children in their care. These teachers reported that, on the average, 75% of the children in their classrooms needed to learn to interact with peers in a more positive and age-appropriate manner. Cooperative learning addresses such concerns. It is easily incorporated into planned, as well as some routine, activities to enhance children's social and emotional growth and skill development. Interestingly, social/emotional functioning is also one of the developmental areas of preschool specifically addressed in the Individuals with Disabilities Education Act (IDEA).

Fostering Prosocial Skills

Cooperative learning has been employed, along with other practices, to increase the development of prosocial behaviors in young children. Prosocial behaviors are those that benefit another person or other organism, and may involve an element of self-sacrifice (Solomon et al., 1985). Some examples of prosocial behaviors are cooperating, compromising, helping, sharing, and telling the truth. A longitudinal study by Daniel Solomon and his colleagues (Solomon et al., 1985; Solomon, Watson, Delucchi, Schaps, and Battistich, 1988) focused on a single cohort of children as it moved from kindergarten through fourth grade. Students in experimental groups participated in a program consisting of five major components: 1) cooperative activities, 2) developmental discipline, 3) activities promoting social understanding, 4) activities highlighting prosocial values, and 5) helping activities. Students in the experimental schools scored significantly higher on two indices of interpersonal behavior—supportive and friendly behavior and spontaneous prosocial behavior—than did students who were not receiving the interventions.

Solomon et al. (1985, p. 390) described the kindergarten curriculum, which contained numerous activities and practices related to each of the five program components:

> For example, when the focus was on helping, the kindergartners made valentines for the parents who work as volunteer aids in their classrooms, made birdfeeders for the school, and worked to help keep parts of the school campus clean. They also learned about and met adult "helpers" in the community, including fire fighters, police, and postal workers. Some kindergartners were paired with fifth- or sixth-grade "buddies," who read to them several times a month, thus providing positive examples of helping.

The use of cooperative learning activities was gradually increased throughout the year, and these activities were structured to involve resource, goal, or reward interdependence. Children frequently engaged in cooperative games and play activities. Books were selected to reinforce prosocial behaviors; for example, "Rudolph the Red-Nosed Reindeer" became the basis for the discussion about teasing.

The study of the effects of cooperative learning on young children in early childhood settings is still in its infancy and begs greater attention from researchers. The questions to be addressed could include the following: What effects does cooperative learning have on young children's cognitive development, social skill development, and perspective-taking abilities? And how should cooperative activities be modified for preschool children?

PLANNING AND CONDUCTING COOPERATIVE
LEARNING ACTIVITIES IN EARLY CHILDHOOD SETTINGS

Cooperative learning should be a part of a teacher's repertoire of pro-
gramming strategies. Bricker and Cripe (1992) identified the three types
of activities that an early childhood program comprises. *Routine activities*
". . . occur on a predictable or regular basis, such as meals, diapering,
and dressing at home; and snacks, clean-up, and preparation for departure at center-based programs" (p. 44). *Planned activities* are "designed
events that ordinarily do not happen without adult organization. Planned
activities should interest children and be developed in ways that children
find appealing, as opposed to being designed exclusively to practice a target skill" (p. 44). Finally, *child-initiated* activities are those generated by
children themselves (p. 44). Early childhood programs usually include a
mix of all three types of activities. However, some children with disabilities do not typically interact with their peers. These children often do not
seek out other children in play situations, and some may actually avoid
interaction with other children. Other children may lack the skills to enter into or maintain interactions. These children may receive special education services in the form of activity-based intervention (ABI) as described by Bricker and Cripe (1992), or through other activities, some of
which may include cooperative learning.

True cooperation seldom occurs spontaneously. Hence, teachers
have an important role in facilitating cooperative learning activities. They
need to remember that the essence of classroom cooperation is transmit-
ted through the coordination, negotiation, and compromises of children
themselves. Asking or telling young children to cooperate is like asking or
telling them to sit still. It may result in mere compliance, but that is not
the goal of cooperative learning. Instead, the teacher must provide opportunities for cooperation, teach cooperative skills, monitor the children's efforts, and provide feedback. This teacher–child interaction is the
same for young children in elementary grades. Although teachers should
minimize their involvement in children's cooperative learning activities,
they do need to keep a watchful eye on how things are going and intervene when necessary.

The Teacher's Role

Select the Activity   Much of the work in setting up cooperative
learning activities takes place during the planning phase. The teacher's
first step is to make a decision about which activities are suitable for cooperative learning groups. The activity selected should be developmentally appropriate for, and motivating to, the children participating. A

knowledge of the children's interests should guide task selection. The second step is to explain the activity to the children and to make sure that they understand what is to be done and what the goals of the activity are.

The selected activity for young children should be fairly simple and straightforward. Many of the cooperative learning activities used with older children are too complex for preschoolers. For example, a "jigsaw" lesson that requires each group member to work individually on a particular aspect of the task and then report what they have done or learned to the group would be difficult for young children as would an activity that lasts for several hours, or one with difficult roles for each member to assume. Foyle, Lyman, and Lyman (1990) give excellent examples of cooperative activities geared toward young children, such as making a peanut butter sandwich, using pattern blocks, and making an Easter-egg mobile.

Delineate a Clear Group Goal   Children need to know what they are supposed to accomplish in their groups. An activity is not cooperative if the children feel no need to coordinate their plans, make decisions, and solve problems together to complete the activity. The children should have the attitude that they will sink or swim together. If they can work individually, even though they are sitting close together or side-by-side and talking while accomplishing the task, then the activity is not necessarily cooperative.

A good test of childrens' understanding is to ask them what they will be doing in the group activity. If they can explain the goal, then it is likely that they understand what they are doing. Actually demonstrating cooperative learning to young children through a puppet demonstration, or letting them watch videotapes or observe cooperative learning/play activities is very helpful. Following the observation, discuss with the children what the groups did to "work together" or "cooperate."

Ensure Individual Responsibility   The participation and contributions of all group members are essential to the success of a cooperative learning activity. Children who are reluctant to participate may be offered a choice of two tasks, such as doing the pasting or the folding. Sometimes children will assume different responsibilities within the group, such as one child being responsible for coloring with the markers and another for cutting out the picture. However, to ensure that they coordinate their ideas and activities, both children should be involved in deciding what picture they will draw and what title they will give it.

Teach Cooperative Skills   In planning cooperative learning, the teacher selects activities that encourage the development of cooperative skills—social skills that are used in group situations. Social skills that are developmentally appropriate for preschool children should be introduced, such as "sharing," "staying with your group or partner," "taking turns," "saying nice things to others," "listening," and "helping."

Kagan (1991) noted that for young children, social skills are the curriculum. "If in the youngest grades, students learn to support and encourage each other, listen carefully to the ideas of others, and work quietly and efficiently in groups, then they have received instruction most predictive of future academic and life success" (p. 5).

Teachers can introduce the skills through the following steps:

1. *Identify* the skill—give it a name.
2. Explain *why* the skill is needed.
3. *Demonstrate* the skill through modeling, explanation, puppet play, videotape, or role play.
4. Ask the children to *use* the skill in their cooperative activity.
5. *Observe* the group activity.
6. Provide *feedback* on how the children are cooperating.

In order not to overwhelm young children, only one skill should be introduced at a time. Practice on a specific collaborative skill may continue over several weeks. Curran (1991) suggests following an informal approach that involves choosing a "social skill of the week." When asked to demonstrate a cooperative skill, children's behavior may seem awkward and artificial at first, but over time the skill will be internalized and become a natural part of the child's behavioral repertoire.

Observe and Provide Feedback   While children are working or playing cooperatively, it is important that the teacher intervene as infrequently as possible. Children need to have genuine opportunities to coordinate their actions and make their own decisions. Because they tend to defer to adult authority, too much teacher direction or intrusion can undermine children's cooperative behaviors and problemsolving initiatives.

As teachers observe children working together, they focus on the interactions, taking note of the specific cooperative skills displayed, and of those in need of improvement. When significant problems that the children are unable to solve arise, the teacher should, of course, provide assistance.

At the end of an activity, it is important to discuss with the children how they cooperated, giving specific feedback and encouragement. During this time, children can describe what they feel they did well and what they need to practice in the future.

Tips for Planning Successful Cooperative Activities

In modifying cooperative learning and play activities for young children, their developmental levels and needs should be taken into account. Listed below are some general suggestions for planning successful cooperative lessons with young children:

Planning the Activity   The more interesting cooperative activi-ties are, the more motivated the children will be to work together. The instructor should observe children to determine their interests and ques-tion them directly about what they like to do. Novelty is also a motivation enhancer.

Select an activity that involves a shared goal, one that requires inter-active communication and coordination of efforts. Rather than have three children each erect a Lego building independently and then com-bine them into a city, encourage them to work together as a group on one building at a time.

Plan activities in which children receive feedback through visible and immediate results (Tudge & Caruso, 1988). Growing crystals, for example, requires waiting for a relatively long period, but making a milkshake together produces tangible results almost immediately.

Size and Composition of Groups   At the preschool level, groups should be small. Children will work well in pairs or triads. In most cases, groups of four or more are too large.

Group heterogeneity should be maximized. Mix together children of different ability levels, sexes, ethnic and cultural backgrounds, and lan-guage skills. Integrate children with and children without disabilities. Teachers should use their best judgment when assigning children to groups. A child with highly developed social skills may work well with one who needs improvement in this area. For manipulative activities, a child with good fine motor abilities can act as a good complement to a child with cerebral palsy.

Teachers should also consider pairing preschool children with older children for cooperative learning. Friedman and Koeppel (1990) describe how pre-K children were paired with first graders in a writing workshop. A 15-minute workshop was scheduled twice a week, during which the pre-K children dictated stories about themselves to the first graders, ex-pressing their feelings and concerns, and how they viewed the classroom environment and the first graders. The first graders put the ideas and words into print or drawings. The authors found the writing partnerships to be extremely successful. In addition to forming friendships, the youn-ger children were able to see how ideas and words are put into print, and the first graders gained in self-esteem as they became "superstars" in the eyes of their younger friends:

> With little or no coaxing, the pre-K children had stories to tell. Some preferred to tell their story first and illustrate it afterwards; others needed to draw first, then describe their picture in detail. In an ongoing conferring process, the first graders, pencils in hands, busily took dictation, helped the younger children articulate their thoughts as they dictated and drew, and reread the finished pieces. (Friedman & Koeppel, 1990, p. 67)

Materials that Stimulate Cooperation Before the lesson, make or obtain materials that will stimulate cooperation. Open-ended materials such as puppets, blocks, and water work well, and dramatic-play areas will also foster cooperative ventures. To enhance cognitive development, materials should enable children to handle or "act on" objects and observe the results (Tudge & Caruso, 1988). The availability of too many materials may discourage cooperation; interdependence is ensured when children must share.

Room Arrangement Children should be able to work close enough together to hear each other and to accomplish their goals without disrupting other groups. Adults should be able to circulate around the room to monitor the groups and provide necessary feedback. Proximity is a must for cooperative learning. Tables sometimes separate children too much; they create unnecessary physical and psychological distances.

Empowering Children Assist children in articulating their own goals before they start on an activity. Tudge and Caruso (1988) noted that:

> During early childhood, when children often act first and discuss later, a teacher can play a vital role by helping them clarify their goal before they attempt to solve the problem. A teacher's input can be very important if it helps children make explicit objectives that are only implied in their behavior. (p. 51)

Encourage children to decide for themselves how to reach the goal of an activity; they will learn about others' perspectives in the process. Furthermore, they will gain greater confidence in their abilities to master goals. In cooperative learning, teachers are discouraged from intervening any more than is absolutely necessary.

Orienting Children to Cooperative Learning Share with the children videos and demonstrations of cooperative learning. Most young children have never seen cooperative learning in action. They need to have an understanding of what they are expected to do, and verbal explanations are rarely sufficient. Videos can be very supportive if they demonstrate to children positive examples of cooperative learning, and visits to cooperative programs and classrooms are also helpful.

Teachers also report that it helps to have posters and pictures of children cooperating with each other or exhibiting social skills such as sharing, smiling, and patting one another on the back.

The excellent quarterly publication *Cooperative Learning: The Magazine for Cooperation in Education* describes a variety of cooperative learning resources for teachers, and includes a column, Video Viewpoint, that reviews videotapes on cooperative learning.

The following lesson plan describes a cooperative learning activity that is fairly easy to organize and uses readily available materials.

LESSON PLAN:
A cooperative unit on the story
"Blueberries for Sal"

Lesson objectives: To create a picture depicting the setting of the story *"Blueberries for Sal,"* by Robert McCloskey; to make a blueberry milkshake.

Activities:

Day 1   The teacher will read the story "Blueberries for Sal" to all of the children. Then, the children will be placed in groups with one large piece of paper and a bottle of glue per group. The groups will be asked to create a picture of the story. Each child will be given an envelope of setting items and characters made of construction paper (one envelope has blueberry bushes and Little Sal, another contains rocks and Sal's mother, another trees and Little Bear). Group members will work together, taking turns, with each child gluing on his or her items. They will also name the setting items and the characters, describing in their own words what they think happened in the story.

Day 2   On the next day the group pictures will be displayed and the group members will discuss the story with the teacher. Then, the same cooperative groups will make blueberry milkshakes. Each child in the group will add one premeasured ingredient to the milkshakes (e.g., blueberries, ice cream, milk), with the teacher providing assistance as needed. The teacher will help the groups blend their ingredients in a blender. Then the children will drink the milkshakes. Adults will be needed to assist the groups, but it is possible to stagger the use of the blenders so that each group doesn't need adult assistance all the time.

Time allotted: 2 class periods.

Materials: Large pieces of paper or poster board and construction-paper cut-outs of characters and setting elements; blender, cups, milk, ice cream, and blueberries.

Heterogeneous groups: The teacher will assign children to groups of three, striving for heterogeneity and a mix of abilities.

Positive interdependence: Each child contributes to the picture and the milkshakes; without the individual pieces and ingredients, the whole would be incomplete.

Individual accountability: Each child will be held accountable for contributing pieces or an ingredient; each child will talk about the story.

Criteria for success: Each group must produce one completed picture and a milkshake for each member.

Cooperative skills: The targeted social skills are taking turns and staying with the group.

Adaptation for an individual difference: A child with a speech impairment will identify objects on the story board using a combination of sign language and speech.

Evaluation: Did the group create a flannel board picture? Can each child say something about the story? Did the group make a milkshake for each member?

Possible variations: Children could measure the milkshake ingredients themselves; they could paste dried blueberries on their picture; they could act the story out.

Adapted from a lesson by Laurie Steller, Kalispell, Montana.

THE INCLUSION OF YOUNG CHILDREN WITH
CHALLENGING NEEDS THROUGH COOPERATIVE ACTIVITIES

> Six-year-old Micael sat rocking in a corner of the child care center the morning I first met him. The staff quickly informed me that I shouldn't disturb him, and that advice reflected their approach to programming strategies. During the morning, other children wandered over to Micael from time to time, but did not try to interact with him, and he seemed unaware of them. Micael has autism and other related disabilities. In a typical early childhood setting, Micael will make no effort on his own to interact with other people or with materials.

We believe that Micael could participate in and benefit from a small group of children engaging in planned activities. Throughout the rest of the chapter, our intention is to provide examples of how this might be possible.

Modifications for Children with Special Needs

When working with young children with special needs, it is not easy to strike the perfect balance between teacher directed one-on-one or group instruction, individualistic learning, and cooperative learning. Teachers first need to capitalize on a child's strengths and capabilities, and then attend to his or her areas of need. Individualized goals can be addressed in many types of learning and play situations, including cooperative ones.

Young children of varying abilities may not work or play together without specific intervention, but it must be understood that children do not have to possess similar physical, cognitive, or communication-ability levels to work together in a productive manner. First, the objective of the activity needs to be determined, and then strategies for adapting the objective to suit the particular needs of a special child should be devised. There are at least five ways in which objectives can be suited to a child with special needs (Putnam, 1991). Using the example of a group of two children preparing a miniature Play-Doh "snack" for another group, with each child being instructed to contribute one type of food item, consider the following types of modifications for students with special needs:

Same Objective—Modified Manner of Response   When discussing what to make for the snack (e.g., cookies or carrots) one child could use a communication board to express himself by pointing to the items that he would like to make. A child without the use of one arm might be assisted with a small rolling pin and cookie cutter. A child without the use of either arm could attempt to mold the Play-Doh with her toes.

Same Objective—Modified Presentation of Material   The objective could remain unchanged, but in order to receive input, the child might need others to use sign language in communicating with him or her. A child with visual impairment might need to be provided with concrete objects in order to conceptualize what the other child desires to make.

Same Objective—Lower Level of Expectations   A child with severe physical disabilities might be able to contribute to the task by patting the Play-Doh or rolling it into a ball.

Same Objective—Reduced Workload   A child who tires easily or is hyperactive might be able to accomplish a portion of the activity (making only one carrot), but could then be allowed to stop or move on to another activity while the group continues.

Personalized Objective   The objective for the child could be unique and could involve working on a functional skill such as grasping and releasing a ball of Play-Doh or practicing mobility by using a scooter board to move to the materials shelf and get the Play-Doh for the activity.

It is important not to rule out cooperative learning just because a child has a disability or is functioning at a lower developmental or cognitive level. Foyle et al. (1990) give examples of cooperative learning lessons designed for the early childhood classroom. They describe how a song such as "Daddy's Taking Us to the Zoo" can be sung cooperatively:

> Different groups of students could sing about different animals in the zoo that are mentioned in the song. Individual students would sing only during their assigned portion of the song. The groups would sing only about different specific animals. The song would provide students with the opportunity to sing as a team and yet learn to wait their turn for part of the song. (p. 1)

A child with a hearing impairment could also participate in this activity if his or her group could learn to sign the refrain and their portion of the song.

Partial participation, in which a child may only do a step or two of an activity, is almost always possible in a cooperative activity. However, teachers must consider what a child will gain from being engaged in a particular activity, and if one activity has little relevance to the child, it is better to choose another. A color-recognition activity may have little relevance to a child who is blind, whereas a building activity with Legos would be more meaningful.

There are numerous ways to adapt a cooperative lesson. What is required is that teachers, parents, paraprofessionals, children, and team members use their individual and collective creativity to generate innovative ideas. (See the cooperative lesson plan, "Blueberries for Sal," on p. 135.)

Difficult Behaviors and Cooperative Learning

If a child exhibits problem behaviors in a cooperative group, teachers must try to understand the origin of the behavior or determine its function. Sometimes the activity is too difficult and the child becomes frustrated. Or the child may not feel well; for example, the behavior may reflect the pain and irritability caused by an ear infection. Or two children who want to possess the same object might engage in a power play that results in a physical struggle. Or a child may want the teacher's attention and slip out the door into the hallway. It is not easy to ascertain why a child is misbehaving, but finding the cause is the first step in addressing the problem.

The most common behavior problem that teachers of young children observe in cooperative groups is nonparticipation, or passivity. When this behavior occurs, prompting peers to encourage participation often fosters increased involvement. Suggesting to one student that she help another select a crayon and then praise him when he does so may be all that is required. Young children often find unique solutions to the behavior problems of their peers. For instance, Tommy has autism and is very reluctant to participate in a cooperative activity. When it is time for cooperative learning, he climbs up to the top of the slide and refuses to come down. Amy's solution is to join Tommy at the top of the slide and go down in a "train" together, making "choo choo" sounds. Then, Tommy is ready to report to their table and begin the project. Also, relatively simple group jobs or roles can be assigned to ensure participation. Danny's job might be to spread the peanut butter in making a peanut butter and jam sandwich.

When young children lack the necessary social skills to cooperate in groups, these skills need to be taught and practiced in group settings. A child who grabs objects from others should be taught the skill of asking for objects, as well as accepting the other child's response or decision. Sharing is also an important social skill for young children to acquire.

Domineering behavior is another common problem. Other children may merely watch while a "take-charge" child does everything. However, the domineering child can be assigned a job that has passive overtones, such as being a "listener" who must follow directions and carry out the suggestions of the other members.

CASE DESCRIPTIONS OF COOPERATIVE
LEARNING IN EARLY CHILDHOOD SETTINGS

The following case descriptions are examples of cooperative learning activities implemented in early childhood settings. They touch upon the topics of scheduling, material selection, technology, and environmental design.

Case #1: Building a Foundation for
Cooperative Activities in a Preschool Program

At first glance, The Children's Center seems to be a typical preschool program. There are several inviting activity centers at the front of the classroom and a couple of others can be seen toward the back. Some children move about freely, while others cluster in small groups. But this is where the similarities with typical programs end.

The Children's Center is designed to support children of differing abilities and to encourage development through cooperative activities. A typical day's schedule would look like this:

  8:15– 8:45 Arrival and free play
  8:45– 9:00 Circle time and planning activities
  9:00– 9:30 Small group time
  9:30– 9:45 Cleanup and preparation for snack
  9:45–10:10 Snack and review
10:15–10:45 Outdoor time
10:45–11:00 Preparation to leave

Posting the schedule in the classroom gives not only staff members, but also visitors, an indication of what to expect. The use of terms such as "planning" and "review," however, indicate that the program follows the High Scope model of "Plan, Do, and Review" (Hohmann, Banet, & Weikart, 1979).

Rick Lee, one of the teachers, puts on a record to signal the end of free play. Amanda Terraut, another teacher, helps two children find a place to store their art project until tomorrow.

After the children are seated in the circle area, Rick begins to tell a story about a little brown hen who wouldn't share, and how the other animals grew to dislike her. After the story, Amanda leads a discussion on sharing. Several children volunteer ways to share materials at the art center.

Sharing is a skill that many children need opportunities to practice. Early in the year Rick and Amanda found that they would need to use various planned activities to introduce many different opportunities for sharing. They decided on several different teaching strategies, including cooperative learning.

When Amanda and Rick asked their students if they knew of any ways to share, the children gave many examples:

Winnie: Sharing is keeping the basket of crayons in the middle of the table.

Anne Marie: Sharing is not using the paste for too long.
Ricardo: Sharing is letting Danny use some of my glue.
Jody: Sharing is taking only one marker at a time.
Jamie: Sharing is passing the crayons when somebody asks.

Amanda drew a sketch of each suggestion and wrote the child's description underneath. The teachers found that the children needed a concrete description of what sharing "looked like" in many different situations. By using the pictures as well as symbols, the children could hang their suggestions on the wall as reminders or points of discussion for another day. Amanda felt that such discussions provided the children with important reference points when carrying out a planned cooperative learning activity.

During the year, Amanda and Rick tried to focus on the following social skills for 4-year-olds:

Sharing
Taking turns
Asking others for help
Being a friend
Listening to others

They used a webbing technique to help to generate ideas for cooperative learning activities that would focus on a particular social skill, as Amanda felt that a visual representation helped her to emphasize the social skill. Figure 1 is a visual representation of the webbing technique used in planning the lesson on the story "Blueberries for Sal."

Davy summed up his impressions as a member of this inclusive program, also attended by 4-year-old Permerika who has cerebral palsy and is nonverbal. Davy reported, "I like doing things together . . . you know why? Permerika can keep a secret!"

Case #2:   Structuring the
Environment To Support Cooperation

In an urban public school, Dick Chan, an early childhood educator, feels that the environment must be a major consideration in promoting cooperative learning activities. His classroom comprises various learning centers, each of which includes three or four chairs. Dick enjoys telling about one of his practicum experiences: The teacher had designed an exciting science area with a hornet's nest, bark from various trees, and a variety of insects to view under different magnifying glasses, but with only one chair! The children in Dick's classroom spend the afternoon on literacy activities. The writing center is one area in which the children work, using different tools (markers and pencils) and paper. A computer with a Muppet Keyboard also sits on the table. Dick explains that the

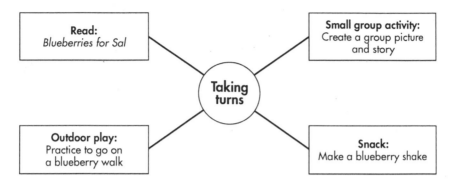

Figure 1.   Planning a cooperative learning activity through the use of webbing.

Muppet Keyboard, which displays the letters in alphabetical order, rather than the usual QWERTY design, is another way to support cooperation among children. The keyboard is attached to the computer with a long cord, so that it can be passed from child to child. Thus, the input is not limited to the one child seated in front of the computer.

Case Study #3: Using Materials To Promote Opportunities for Cooperation

Sandi Hines has been a preschool teacher for 15 years. Currently, she has a morning program of 15 4-year-old children. Sandi has found that not only the environment, but also the materials in the classroom, influence the types of play in which children engage.

One toy that she finds valuable is a wooden rocking boat. The boat has a seat at each end and works best when there is at least one child on each seat. When two children use the boat, they need to rock together in order to get the boat to move up and down; competition simply doesn't work in this situation.

Another favorite—of both teacher and children, Sandi explains—is a colorful circular parachute. Each child grabs hold of a part of the edge; then, by moving their arms up and down in unison, they make the light-weight material billow out. The more children who participate, the easier the task of "flying" the parachute becomes—and the more fun!

Sandi also found that the number of materials she displays in the classroom affects the children's degree of cooperation. For example, in the work area, she includes only two hammers and one screwdriver; thus, the children need to share the tools and cooperate in order to build anything. Sandi has found that children will more readily generalize the skills developed in cooperative learning activities to other activities in the classroom when her plans specify materials that must be used in the activity centers.

CONCLUDING COMMENTS

Cooperation is an essential skill for young and old people alike, and learning how to cooperate should begin in the early childhood years. Consequently, cooperative learning has an important place in early childhood education. For children with challenging needs, it provides an excellent context in which meaningful interaction and learning can take place. Through participation in cooperative activities, children are able to observe the actions of others and to coordinate and negotiate their behaviors with those of others. They can also solve problems, communicate, and have fun at the same time.

Cooperative learning yields the most positive results when children have a shared goal and are active participants in reaching that goal. The social skills necessary for working and playing together are learned in the process. Planned activities incorporating cooperative learning strategies are particularly important for those young children who do not successfully interact with peers.

Cooperative learning takes a lot of planning, patience, and trust in children, but the results are worth the extra effort when one sees how much the achievement and cognitive and social development of young children with and without special needs are enhanced.

REFERENCES

Borke, H. (1973). The development of empathy in Chinese and American children between three and six years of age: A cross cultural study. *Developmental Psychology, 9,* 102–108.

Bricker, D., & Cripe, J.J.W. (1992). *An activity-based approach to early intervention.* Baltimore: Paul H. Brookes Publishing Co.

Cartwright, S. (1987). Group endeavor can be valuable learning in nursery school. *Young Children, 42*(5), 8–11.

Cartwright, S. (1993). Cooperative learning can occur in any kind of program. *Young Children, 48*(2), 75–81.

Curran, L. (1991) *Cooperative learning lessons for little ones: Literature-based language arts and social skills.* San Juan Capistrano, CA: Resources for Teachers.

Damon, W. (1983). *Social and personality development: Infancy through adolescence.* New York: Norton.

Foyle, H.C., Lyman, L., & Lyman, S. (1990, March). *Using cooperative learning in the early childhood classroom.* Paper presented at the Annual Conference of the Association for Supervision and Curriculum Development, San Antonio, TX.

Foyle, H.C., Lyman, L., & Thies, S.A. (1991). *Cooperative learning in the early childhood classroom.* NEA Early Childhood Education Series. Washington, DC, National Education Association.

Friedman, J., & Koeppel, J. (1990). Pre-K and first grade children: Partners in a writing workshop. *Young Children, 45*(4) 66–67.

Goffin, S.G. (1987). Cooperative behaviors: They need our support. *Young Children, 42*(1), 75–81.

Hill, T., & Reed, K. (1990). Promoting social competence at preschool: The implementation of a co-operative games programme. *Early Child Development and Care, 59,* 11–20.

Hohmann, M., Banet, B., & Weikart, D.P. (1979). *Young children in action.* Ypsilanti, MI: High Scope Press.

Johnson, D., & Johnson, R. (1989). *Cooperation and competition: Theory and research.* Edina, MN: Interaction Book Company.

Johnson, D.W., Skon, L., & Johnson, R. (1980). Effects of cooperative, competitive, and individualistic conditions on children's problem-solving performance. *American Educational Research Journal, 17*(1), 83–93.

Kagan, S. (1991). In L. Curran, *Cooperative learning lessons for little ones; Literature-based language arts and social skills.* San Juan Capistrano, CA: Resources for Teachers.

McCloskey, R. (1948/1982). *Blueberries for Sal.* New York: Penguin Books.

Murray, F.B. (1972). Acquisition of conservation through social interaction. *Developmental Psychology, 6,* 1–6.

Odom, S.L., McConnell, S.R., & McEvoy, M.A. (Eds.). (1992). *Social competence of young children with disabilities: Issues and Strategies for Intervention.* Baltimore: Paul H. Brookes Publishing Company

Parten, M.B. (1932). Social participation among preschool children. *Journal of Abnormal Psychology, 27,* 243–269.

Perret-Clermont, A.N. (1980). *Social interaction and cognitive development in children.* Orlando, FL: Academic Press.

Piaget, J. (1951). *Play, dreams, and imitation in childhood.* New York: Norton.

Piaget, J. (1954). *The construction of reality in the child.* New York: Basic Books.

Piaget, J. (1968). *Six psychological studies* (A. Tenzer, Trans.). New York: Vintage Books.

Putnam, J.W. (1991). Curricular adaptations for students with disabilities in co-operative groups. *Cooperative Learning, 12*(1), 10.

Skon, L., Johnson, D.W., & Johnson, R.T. (1981). Cooperative peer interaction versus individual competition and individualistic efforts: Effects on the acquisition of cognitive reasoning strategies. *Journal of Educational Psychology, 36,* 565–572.

Slavin, R.E. (1990). *Cooperative learning: Theory, research and practice.* Englewood Cliffs, NJ: Prentice Hall.

Smilansky, S., & Shefatya, L. (1990). *Facilitating play: A medium for promoting cognitive, socio-emotional and academic development in young children.* Gaithersburg, MD: Psychosocial and Educational Publications.

Solomon, D., Watson, M. Battistich, V., Schaps, E. Tuck, P. Solomon, J., Cooper, C., & Ritchey, W. (1985). A program to promote interpersonal consideration and cooperation in children. In R. Slavin, S. Sharan, S. Kagan, R.H. Lazarowitz, C. Webb, & R. Schmuck (Eds.), *Learning to cooperate, cooperating to learn* (pp. 371–402). New York: Plenum Press.

Solomon, D., Watson, M.S., Delucchi, K.L. Schaps, E., & Battistich, V. (1988). Enhancing children's prosocial behavior in the classroom. *American Educational Research Journal, 25*(4), 527–554.

Tudge, J., & Caruso, D. (1988) Cooperative problem solving in the classroom: Enhancing young children's cognitive development. *Young Children, 43,* 46–52.

7

Cooperative Learning and Cultural Diversity
Building Caring Communities in the Cooperative Classroom

DILAFRUZ R. WILLIAMS

With the rapidly changing demographics in the United States, many schools, particularly urban schools, are undergoing a major ethnic and racial shift in their student populations (Hilliard III, 1991–1992; Hodgkinson, 1985). Hence, one of the pressing duties of educators is responding to the needs, not only of academically diverse students, but also of culturally heterogeneous students, in their classrooms (Fradd & Weismantel, 1990; Sleeter & Grant, 1987). Traditionally, schools have responded to student diversity with pullout and alternative programs, many of which have included an overrepresentation of minorities (Oakes, 1985). However, in recent years, a surge of interest has emerged in inclusive instructional practices such as cooperative learning (Johnson, Johnson, & Holubec, 1988; Slavin, 1990) and multicultural education to address the historical neglect of non-Eurocentric viewpoints in the curriculum (Banks, 1988a).

Since representation of all cultural groups is necessary in a democratic society (Hilliard III, 1991–1992), educational practices that are in-

Development of this chapter was supported in part by the Center for Urban Research in Education and a Faculty Development Grant at Portland State University. No official endorsement should be inferred, however. I wish to acknowledge the assistance of Cynthea Hayakawa with data collection.

clusive, and that address multiculturalism, are crucial. Given the increasing ethnic and cultural diversity in the population, schools are fertile grounds for students to interact with children who are *different* from themselves. However, because many students live in relatively isolated pockets of neighborhoods that prevent interaction among people of different cultures, they may come to school with stereotypes about other cultural and ethnic groups, and this may sometimes result in conflicts. Nonetheless, we can reasonably assume that schools provide significant opportunities for raising cultural awareness and understanding, and for the formation of caring communities, perhaps more so than any other setting, especially because schools are an environment in which youngsters spend at least 6 hours a day together in one stable setting. It is when students from different cultures begin to interact with and get to know one another in a supportive classroom environment that they can learn to recognize stereotypes and their associated prejudices and begin to address them.

In this chapter, the highlights of events and lessons used by an urban middle school teacher are presented to demonstrate the possibilities of several inclusive, multicultural practices. In caring for her students and building communities in her academically and culturally diverse classroom, the teacher, Ms. Penrose, is an inspiration for others. Although Ms. Penrose taught 30 8th graders, the examples are sufficiently detailed to allow them to be adapted and modified for use by teachers at the elementary and high school levels.

First, the multicultural context and classroom environment of Ms. Penrose and her students are presented. Next, the features of a "community," drawn from the literature on the formation of communities and the essence of caring, are discussed. An argument is also made for the importance of the elements of the Johnson and Johnson model of cooperative learning, which have the potential to help teachers to build and nurture caring communities in the classroom. This argument leads into concrete examples and strategies for the formation of communities in the cooperative classroom.

One such method that is described in this chapter is a cooperative lesson designed to teach students the necessity of working together to achieve goals unattainable by any individual working alone. In addition, student interpretations of the value of cooperative learning are illustrated by their responses to an evaluative activity designed both to develop their abilities to write persuasive essays and to promote reflection on the value of cooperation. Other examples are also given, including methods for teaching critical thinking through group analysis of television and other media to demonstrate how they portray racism and sexism and for using multicultural materials to broaden students' perspectives.

A MULTICULTURAL CLASSROOM CONTEXT

Let's listen to the voices of four urban 8th graders who demonstrated not only awareness but also acceptance of cultural diversity during a year spent with their teacher, Ms. Penrose, who subscribed to an ethic of care and cooperation in her diverse classroom:

> You don't dislike a person because he happens to be Mexican or white, because he is a different color. See how they feel inside, not how they look outside.
>
> —Lorenzo Rodriguez, Hispanic

> Diversity means how you are different from one another. Well, everybody is different in some ways. My grandmother always used to tell me, no one's ugly. She's always telling, God didn't make nobody ugly. 'Cuz what's in you is not in someone else and that's your unique. And now, Ms. Penrose made me realize that cooperative learning teaches you to see strength [in that] which is unique in each one of us.
>
> —Temekia Johnson, African American

> Students stereotype one another. People I thought were different—with different skin color and not like me, wearing certain kinds of clothing, talking in a different way or sometimes a different language, I didn't know how to approach. But now, a year later, those same students are my friends. Working in groups and learning to cooperate helped me to understand that I had stereotyped those same students who are my friends now. You kinda have to know how to approach others, learn to deal with differences, instead of making fun of them.
>
> —John Parker, Caucasian

> In my culture it is important to keep the chain of friendship connected, in spite of someone being mean and trying to break it. I try to be tolerant when someone makes fun of my English or accent. We have to deal with differences by talking to one another in order to clear our misunderstandings. Only then can we continue the chain of friendship.
>
> —Mounty Nguyen, Asian

These views unfolded in an 8th-grade classroom in a large inner-city middle school. Lorenzo, Temekia, John, Mounty, and their 26 classmates belonged to Ms. Penrose's core class. For four periods daily, they were absorbed in studying English and social studies and, during what was referred to as "the advisory period," discussing and resolving their personal problems as a class with Ms. Penrose. While the academic rites of schooling are experienced by millions of students in American classrooms, Ms. Penrose's teaching methods were atypical. Over a period of 10 months she was immersed in a philosophy of education that stresses the importance of building a caring community in the classroom.

The significance of this uncommon venture becomes evident when we examine the constitution of Ms. Penrose's class. As in many urban schools, her class of 30 adolescents consisted of a culturally diverse mix of African Americans, Native Americans, Hispanic Americans, and Asians (Hmong, Cambodian, Vietnamese, East-Indian, and Malaysian). Language and race differences were conspicuous in the student body, but there were also academic differences that were not so evident. Although many of her students were classified as needing remediation, Ms. Penrose had worked out an arrangement with the school administrators whereby none of her students was pulled out for special services. A majority of the students were of low socioeconomic status and many came from homes that were described as dysfunctional. The school itself was located in a neighborhood in which violence and drug dealing were problems.

Ms. Penrose, who is white, had 10 years of experience teaching adolescents. She had tried cooperative learning 5 years earlier and became "hooked on it." She explained that education was more meaningful to her students when they were "engaged in caring and cooperative behaviors that were not often modeled by others in their lives outside of school." Ms. Penrose was known widely within the school for her adoption of the Johnson and Johnson model of cooperative learning (Johnson et al., 1988), and her teaching was characterized by much zest and vigor as she herself demonstrated an attitude of care and concern for her students. Of course, her challenge was not only to motivate the students academically, but also to help them to overcome a sense of despair, to learn to deal with differences and address racism, and to establish and maintain their "chain of friendship," the fitting metaphor used by one of Ms. Penrose's students, Mounty Nguyen.

FEATURES OF CARING COMMUNITIES
AND THE ROLE OF COOPERATIVE LEARNING

One way to clarify what is meant by "caring communities" and to learn how they can be formed in classrooms is to turn to the literature on the formation of communities (Benne, 1989; Dewey, 1916; Green, 1984; Noddings, 1984). Consider, for instance, the constitutive elements of a community: membership, communication, interaction and mutual dependence, common and shared experiences, attachment and bonding, internalization of a set of norms and moral standards, and an ethic of concern for members of the group. In his classic book, *Democracy and Education*, Dewey (1916) writes:

> There is more than a verbal tie between the words common, community, and communication. Mèn live in a community by virtue of things they have in common; and communication is the way in which they come to possess things in common. What they have in common in order to form a community . . . are aims, beliefs, aspirations, knowledge—a common understanding. (p. 4)

Community, for Dewey, denotes a group of individuals who have shared interests and who mutually pursue the common good. One cannot impose membership on an individual. Rather, communities come into being because individual members come together to pursue common interests. In keeping with this notion of community, Raywid (1989) finds these features to be conditions that help "the shaping of individual identity, an acceptance of group standards and a desire to abide by them, commitment, a sense of place, and identification with a group, along with a consciousness of a kind" (p. 3). How might cooperative learning promote such a consciousness?

Unlike the traditional individualistic model of instruction, cooperative learning not only permits, but indeed requires, communication among group members while they work on academic tasks. Students are expected to interact with one another as they take on roles, collectively engage in solving problems, explain their thinking to one another, and discuss ways to resolve conflicts that may arise. Merely adhering to the principle of majority rule is not acceptable when dealing with differences; common understandings are arrived at only when the individuals in a group are able to present their points of view and to discuss their perspectives on problems. Positive interdependence, individual accountability, interaction, communication, and discussion are necessary features of cooperative learning. Thus, students learn to deal with differences, recognize each other's strengths, show respect by acknowledging the contributions of all group members to the task at hand, take turns, and, in the process of sharing their experiences, gain the practical experience of dealing with peers who are neither culturally nor academically like themselves. This sense of mutual trust and openness is possible only when students are given opportunities to attend to tasks collectively, that is, when cooperation, rather than competition, is the classroom norm.

EXAMPLES OF LESSONS

In this section, two examples demonstrate different ways of dealing with diversity in the classroom. The first is a fable with a moral that teaches a valuable lesson. The fable can be acted out in class by students. The second is a lesson plan that demonstrates how cooperative learning can be used in a good opening-of-the-year activity. The purpose is to help students recognize differences among themselves so that they can begin to accept them. (These lessons, which have been slightly adapted, were developed by three middle school teachers, Bonnie Lang, Nedra Russell, and Gail Halpern, as part of the Syracuse Stay in School Partnership Project. This project was funded by the New York State Education Department as a collaborative effort between Syracuse University and the Syracuse [NY] City School District. See Williams [1990] for further information. Manuals are available from Luanna H. Meyer, Ph.D., School of Education, Syracuse University, Syracuse, New York 13244.)

The Use of Fables

Narratives have tremendous possibilities in terms of communicating to students the importance of working together without putting one another down. Students are likely to occasionally indulge in stereotypes that are associated with race and culture, and may even use racial slurs in the classroom. Learning to cooperate is not an easy task, especially when many instructional practices encourage competitiveness and individual work. The following narrative was used by Ms. Penrose when she found that disruption of the group process caused students in her class to put each other down, hurl racial insults, stay off-task, and not pay attention to their roles. It was particularly effective because of the follow-up discussion and analysis period.

A Bundle of Sticks:
A Fable about Cooperative Learning

Setting:	*A class using the Johnsons' model of cooperative learning with three members per group.*
Narrator:	There once was a teacher who wanted her students to help each other learn and to respect each other's differences. When she put her students into groups one day, this is what happened.
Teacher:	Before you begin your task today, I would like each of you to tell me what your role is and what your task will be.
Narrator:	The students explained their roles as checker, recorder, and facilitator/ leader. The students seemed to work well for a few minutes. Soon, however . . .
Leader:	I'm not sure how to do this question.
Checker:	Well, I'm not surprised.
Leader:	Well, you are so ugly the doctor slapped you when you were born.
Recorder:	You guys are sure good at making digs, but we need to dig into this work if we are going to complete it on time.
Checker:	Even if we were to help you, it wouldn't do any good. You're so slow it takes you two hours to watch "60 Minutes."
Recorder:	Who needs you guys! I'm going to do the work by myself. *(Moves desk away from the group.)*
Narrator:	Then the teacher came to the group carrying a bundle of sticks.
Teacher:	Which of you can break this bundle?
Narrator:	Each student tried, but no one could break the bundle. *A student passes the bundle to a nearby peer saying, "I give up. Here Rick, you try." Rick also fails. Then the teacher unties bundle and hands a stick to each student in the group.*
Teacher:	Now see if you can break this. *As each student breaks a stick they say such things as, "Oh, it's a snap, . . . a "piece of cake" . . . "easy!"*

Teacher:	Each of you alone is fragile. Each of you has feelings as easy to injure as one of these sticks. But if you are friendly and stick together, you will be as strong as the sticks were when they were tied in a bundle.
Leader:	Oh, I get it. If we work together without making nasty comments, we'll do better.
Checker:	Yeah, like a buddy system.
Recorder:	I would rather work together than learn this stuff by myself, anyway. (*Moves her desk back into the group formation.*)
Narrator:	All three students in the group slap hands.
Leader:	Dive in buddies!
Narrator:	The group didn't live happily ever after following this class, but they did *learn* together more happily because they cut out the put-downs and insults and tried to build up each other's strengths instead.

Follow-up class discussion questions:

What happened when the leader asked for help?

How do you think the students felt when being insulted?

What did the students do in response to put-downs? Why?

What would have been an appropriate response to the leader's request for help?

What is the logical solution to a problem that students have trouble solving individually?

This fable can be enacted by the whole class or it can be conducted by the teacher with a particular group that is not working well. The entire class can engage in discussing the many questions associated with this fable.

Cooperative Interviews

This is a good start-of-the-year activity. It can also be used to generate sensitivity toward students who do not belong to the mainstream culture. The interview sheet can be modified to accommodate students of different ages and grade levels.

Students interview each other in pairs, filling in an interview sheet (see Figure 1); partners then introduce each other to the rest of the class. The interview sheet should focus on the particulars of the student's appearance, background, personal preferences, and individuality. Students who have different languages can also be requested to say or write a few words in those languages. Every effort should be made to generate a feeling of interest for that which is different, and the teacher should emphasize how rich the classroom is because of its diversity.

STUDENT PERCEPTIONS OF COOPERATIVE LEARNING

Ms. Penrose, working with a colleague, used the subject of cooperative learning itself as an assignment in her language arts classes. After the

---

Interview Sheet

Materials needed: One interview sheet per student.
Time required: Two class periods.
Group size: 2 (If there is an odd number of students in the class, the teacher should join the group.)

Your Name: _____
1. What is your partner's name? _____
    What is the color of her skin? _____ Her hair? _____
    Her eyes? _____
2. How old is she? _____
3. Where was she born? _____
    If she was not born in USA, when did she immigrate to this coun-
    try? _____
    How does she feel about it? _____
    _____
    _____
    _____
4. What is her first language? _____
    In her language, what is the word for "friend?" _____
5. Where does she live? _____
6. What sorts of things does she care about in school? _____
    _____
    Outside of school? _____
    _____
7. What kind of pets does she have? _____
8. What is her favorite subject? _____
    Her favorite TV show? _____
    What does she like about it? _____
    _____
    _____
9. What type of music does she like to listen to? _____
    What is her favorite group? _____
10. What does she want to be when she graduates from school? ___
    _____
11. Are there any other questions that you would like to ask? (Sugges-
    tion: In what ways do you find your partner's culture different from
    your own? Similar to your own?) _____
    _____
    _____

Figure 1. Interview Sheet

students were taught how to write persuasive essays, they were asked to write an essay on how they felt about cooperative learning and why they felt as they did, and to persuade readers of the essays to accept their position. Listening to students' voices is extremely important in determining what does and doesn't work when cooperative learning is used (Matthews, 1992; Sapon-Shevin, 1993). The various benefits of cooperative learning mentioned by students in Ms. Penrose's class, related to both academic tasks and social interaction, can be classified as follows:

Opportunities To Experience Different Approaches to Learning and a Variety of Answers Cooperative learning was seen by many students as providing opportunities for them to learn in "many different ways." One student wrote, "In groups we can have more than one answer or opinion on questions; when we don't understand the teacher, and a peer explains in different words, it helps a lot." Other students expressed their feelings as follows: "We learn new things from other students' ideas," and "Kids in my group might have different opinions than others. Some might agree and some might disagree; but they can tell *why* to help others understand." Yet another student explained, "[students] can interact with different types of people, they can work with everyone, they can give and receive help from other students. They express their feelings, they get more than one point of view."

Peer/Social Interaction and Sharing One could infer that a majority of the essays revolved around the opportunity for peer interaction, which is particularly essential for adolescents. Some of the statements in favor of cooperative learning were as follows:

> You get to talk to kids; there's a lot of eye contact, which shows that students really care. . . .

and:

> I am for group work because kids can help each other gain confidence in themselves. Other students help praise one another, also helping each other when it's needed and don't put each other down as much. So I really think group work is very important. Lots of kids gain hope and their confidence gets higher . . . it's good to have someone your age to care and help to show adults that kids working in groups can get the job done. . . .

Those that liked cooperative learning felt that they could share ideas in groups; that they sometimes learned to "compromise" in the process if someone else was more convincing; and that big projects got done best when tasks were discussed and problems were solved together.

Writing about respect and caring, some students noted, "If one has low self-esteem . . . when they come into a group their self-esteem and work progress," and "students . . . respect their group members and are constructive." Sensitive to a newcomer, one student wrote: "Say for example somebody is new and doesn't know anyone well. They need to work in a group so they can get to know others."

More Fun During Learning A number of students found this opportunity to communicate with peers and put their heads together to resolve problems to be "more fun" than traditional classroom activities.

Free Ride, Goofing Off, Time-On-Task Concerns   These problems were seen as the most serious by those students who disliked cooperative learning, as well as by those who liked it but with reservations. Some kids "just goof off"—talk, disrupt the group process, or do not contribute anything, yet still enjoy the benefits of the group. "Free ride" was an issue across performance levels, not just for the high-achieving students, as is often claimed. Those who preferred to work by themselves complained:

> I don't enjoy working in groups because I don't get as much done as when I work by myself. Some students start to play and talk and we don't get it [the work] done.

The fact that some students were "bossy" was a fairly common complaint. One low-achieving student explained,

> I enjoy working in groups some of the time . . . but a lot of the time the people I work with act up and tend to be bossy.

Yet, some students acknowledged,

> I really like working in groups more than I don't like working in groups. It's a privilege to work in groups more than not to work in them at all . . . If I was not working in a group today, I would not be working today.

If many students goof off then it takes longer to complete a task. Although this was the greatest concern for the high achievers, a number of students also expressed the idea that when students seriously attended to the tasks, "work got done faster" when done in groups.

Quality of Work   Many students indicated that they liked cooperative learning because the work got done not only faster, but also, better, due to the advantage of discussions with other group members. "I have the benefit of four brains, instead of only one, when I work in groups," was a typical response. However, for a few students, individual efforts appeared to result in more productivity, which they tended to associate with improved quality of work.

Future Benefits/Disadvantages   Among the benefits discussed were the following: "There are hardly any jobs in the world where you work alone;" and "working in groups makes kids grow to like working and helps them develop a positive attitude and outlook on group work." Although "We can get better grades" was another benefit communicated by most students, a few felt that their grades were affected negatively by cooperative learning. Among other disadvantages was the impression that the use of cooperative learning at the middle school level did not prepare adolescents for high school or college. This criticism reflects an image of high school and college environments in which competitiveness is the acceptable norm. Furthermore, one student wrote,

> I enjoy working in both groups and alone. I think we should keep working in groups because that would help the children get used to working with other children. Children need to feel good working with other children, they need to feel like they can trust other children. [But] it would be healthy also to let children work alone . . . [since they] need to know how to depend on themselves also. They need to have a chance to make it happen on their own.

Ms. Penrose used these responses to discuss in class how the students felt about learning with one another. Realizing that the discrepancies seen by some students were couched in terms of the difference between their own work and the minimal involvement of others, Ms. Penrose began to address these problems with the students. Although much of what the class had written about cooperative learning had been positive, a certain amount of unhappiness with the inequalities of work input was demonstrated by some students. Inequalities, therefore, needed to be addressed and resolved. The injustice epitomized by the "free ride" that some students got away with also had to be tackled. Ms. Penrose immediately began to use an evaluation form with each group to provide immediate feedback on how group members perceived their own activities and interactions in the group in such areas as contributing ideas, praising and helping others, and staying on task. While the problem was not completely resolved by the end of the year, her approach was encouraging. It enabled students to view their own interactions critically and to discuss their group dynamics openly among themselves; many students began to realize how differently people could perceive the same event. Moreover, with better monitoring, Ms. Penrose was able to attend to the problem of "free riders" by talking individually to them and helping them to see the unfairness of not sharing in the group's work.

ANALYZING MEDIA MATERIALS/TV SHOWS

It is very important for children to become aware of how different groups are portrayed in the media with regard to culture, race, gender, class, or disabling condition. For teachers at various grade levels, the daily newspaper and television can be rewarding resources for teaching critical thinking, deductive reasoning, separation of facts from opinions, examination of statistics, and sensitivity toward others.

Ms. Penrose, for instance, developed a cooperative learning lesson based on the critical examination of advertisements in the media—both print and television. In this lesson, different groups focused on different aspects of the advertisements: Who is portrayed? What ethnic groups/

races are represented? How is beauty symbolized? How are women portrayed? What do the advertisements say about the various social and economic classes? Groups then shared their responses with the entire class.

Some cooperative groups were assigned to examine articles and photographs in the newspaper on people who were poor and/or homeless. Juxtaposing the two themes—advertisements symbolizing materialism and an image of the world captured in the photographs of poverty —resulted in a class project that was displayed on the bulletin board. The sensitivity of the class was often expressed in the form of poems and essays written by the different cooperative groups.

In addition, day-to-day events have new meaning to young people as they begin to understand the stereotypes that are perpetuated by the media. Gender stereotypes are of particular interest once students begin to critically assess how women are portrayed in soap operas, newscasts, and talk shows. Discussing gender roles and expectations also helps students to examine their own assumptions, values, and beliefs.

Moreover, students can learn to critically assess various types of published information. For instance, the discussions concerning race and gender led students to examine the manner in which the textbooks they used in their social studies and English classes portrayed women and people of color; the students began to explore and discuss as a class how gender and race roles were represented, as well as what groups were left out entirely. Their examination of stories and poems, along with accompanying pictures, made them conscious of the white culture having been predominantly represented in many sources. Eventually, some of the students began to bring articles from the daily newspaper that presented race-related issues. These were handled sensitively as the class as a whole inspected and scrutinized the materials. Such whole-class involvements in discussions and critical analysis are important for nurturing the formation of community among the class.

A cooperative classroom is impossible to create unless there is mutual respect and caring among its members. Individuals need to care enough about diversity to value people who are unlike themselves. When students become aware of their own prejudices and question their own images of ethnicity, gender, or race, an environment of trust and openness can be developed in the classroom.

DEVELOPING MULTICULTURAL LITERACY

Given that cultural diversity is a factor that all educators must contend with, particularly in urban schools, there has been a surge of writing and interest in "multicultural education" in recent years. (Terms such as multicultural education, multiethnic education, and education for cultural pluralism are used to denote the same overall goals and objectives of dealing with heterogeneity and pluralism in American education [Banks, 1988a, 1988b; Gay, 1988, 1990; Sleeter & Grant, 1987].) It must be recognized that the entire context of schooling—curriculum, structure, instructional materials, teaching style, testing and assessment, and so on, has been addressed under the rubric of "multicultural education" (Banks, 1988a) as urban school populations become more diverse in terms of their ethnic and racial composition. Many approaches to multicultural education have been proposed, with different philosphical orientations, ranging from single-group studies, to a view toward enhancing human relations among cultures, to educating for social reconstructionism (Sleeter & Grant, 1987).

Recognizing that not much of the mainstream curriculum addresses multicultural literacy, teachers at all levels have taken to supplementing textbooks with multicultural poems, essays, stories, and games. If cooperative learning is to foster caring communities in the classroom, teachers should make time to prepare lessons and cooperative activities that expose children to an environment in which differences are recognized and celebrated.

James Banks (1988a) provides a useful framework for understanding how to achieve such an environment in practice. Banks presents a variety of paradigms about multiculturalism—*ethnic additive, cultural deprivation, racism, radicalism, cultural pluralism, cultural differences,* and *assimilation.* It is the *cultural differences* paradigm that is most relevant to this discussion, because its major goal is to "change the school so that it respects and legitimizes the cultures of students from diverse ethnic groups and cultures" (Banks, 1988a, p. 97). Based on the assumption that "minority youths have rich and diverse cultures that have values, languages, and behavioral styles that are functional for them and valuable for the nation-state" (p. 97), Banks proposes educational practices that "incorporate their cultures when developing instructional principles, and that integrate ethnic content into the mainstream curriculum" (p. 97).

Several levels of multicultural education were assessed by Banks (1988b): 1) the *contributions approach,* which is most popular, adds ethnic heroes (seldom heroines) and includes celebrating the popular ethnic holidays; 2) the *ethnic additive approach* involves the addition to the curriculum of relevant content, materials, themes, and topics without changing the curricular content's structure, purpose, and nature; 3) the *transformation approach* involves including a variety of perspectives on the same topic in the curriculum; and 4) the *decisionmaking and social action approach* takes students to a level on which they not only gather pertinent multicultural materials, but also analyze their own values and beliefs, examine their stereotypes and prejudices, identify alternatives, decide what actions to take to attain these alternatives, and ultimately aim at reducing discrimination and prejudices. It is important that when teachers plan cooperative learning their lessons be embedded in materials that progress in such a way as to not let them get caught up in doing what many newcomers to the field of multicultural education end up doing—indulging in only the first two levels charted by Banks (1988b).

Ms. Penrose and other teachers of English have used many multicultural materials, such as poems, short stories, essays, biographies, and songs, that touch the core of their students' lives. Such materials serve as a bouncing board for teachers who are interested in making their students, as well as themselves, literate about other cultures. Below are some examples of the decision-making and social action approach.

Poems   There are a number of poems that can serve as rich materials that capture children's imagination about other cultures and provide an enriching departure point for discussions of one's own prejudices and stereotypes about other races and cultures. For example, "Indian Children Speak" (Bell, 1975), "The Negro Mother" (Hughes, 1975), and "To Look at Anything" (Moffitt, 1975), have helped many students in this direction. Each of these poems provides a distinct voice of another culture and encourages the reader to pause and assess his or her own conditioning about other cultures. As representative of how this might happen, the poem "Indian Children Speak" captures the essence of how whites interpret the actions of a nonwhite child, and how different that interpretation is from what the actions mean to the Indian children themselves. The poem also presents the role of nature and the connection of certain cultures to the earth, which very few have appreciated. On reading such poems, cooperative groups can interpret the meanings and begin to question how they have viewed what somebody has done or said, and whether there can be different interpretations of the world based on one's cultural nucleus.

In yet another instance, Steinbergh (1991) showed how children can be encouraged to write their own poems, even in their own languages. Letting recent immigrants talk about their homelands also generates an interest in other lands and cultures, and in other children, something that Ms. Penrose believed was important for the development of sensitivity and caring. Personal expressions such as poems are likely to engender understanding and sympathy toward newcomers, as well as an appreciation of cooperative learning because of the opportunities that the method provides for communication and inclusion.

Short Stories Many multicultural short stories provide alternative scenarios and visions not commonly available in the traditional mainstream curriculum and instruction. Stories such as "The Children of Sanchez" (Lewis, 1975) and "The Boy Who Painted Christ Black" (Clarke, 1975) not only provide voices of other cultures that children can begin to relate to, but they also enable them to pause and wonder about how their own experiences differ from those of the Hispanic and African American children captured in the two stories. Ms. Penrose handled such stories with great sensitivity. As an example, she used "The Boy Who Painted Christ Black," which is an inspirational tale of an African American boy who had the courage and artistic freedom to paint Christ black. The story teaches students the realities of racism and can engage them in critical thinking. However, while these serve as representative examples of Banks's (1988b) transformation and decision-making approaches, these materials must be handled with care and sensitivity, and should lead to cooperative group work and whole-class discussions. A cooperative classroom atmosphere can be generated with such supplemental materials, which are often available in local libraries. These materials can be used to develop sensitivity, empathy, and literacy about other cultures. The goal should be to move away from the mere celebration of ethnic holidays to substantive discussions of the issues surrounding cultural differences.

CONCLUDING COMMENTS

This chapter presented scenarios, proposals, and examples to illustrate how caring communities can be built in the heterogeneous classroom using cooperative learning as an instructional strategy. Children of all ages can be taught to value the richness of cultural differences. To facilitate children's acceptance of such differences, teachers should provide materials that are multicultural and that generate sensitivity toward others. Furthermore, children need to be taught to be introspective, to think critically about their own stereotypes and prejudices, and to share with one another their diverse perspectives. Insofar as cooperative learning requires that students interact with one another and communicate, there is potential not only for creating inclusive environments in the classroom, but also for rooting our educational system in the realities of modern America's diversity.

REFERENCES

Banks, J.A. (1988a). *Multiethnic education: Theory and practice* (2nd ed.). Newton, MA: Allyn & Bacon.

Banks, J.A. (1988b). Approaches to multicultural curriculum reform. *Multicultural Leaders, 1*(2), 17–18.

Bell, J. (1975). Indian children speak. In L. Haupt L. Heston, & S. Solotaroff (Eds.), *Literature lives* (p. 21). Evanston, IL: McDougal, Littel & Co.

Benne, K.D. (1989). If schools are to help build communities. In J. Giarelli (Ed.), *Philosophy of education* (pp. 18–24). Normal, IL: Philosophy of Education Society.

Clarke, J.H. (1975). The boy who painted Christ black. In L. Haupt L. Heston, & S. Solotaroff (Eds.), *Literature lives* (pp. 27–33). Evanston, IL: McDougal, Littel & Co.

Dewey, J. (1916). *Democracy and education*. New York: The Free Press.

Fradd, S., & Weismantel, M. (1990). *Meeting the needs of culturally and lingustically different students*. Boston: Little, Brown.

Gay, G. (1988). Designing relevant curricula for diverse learners. *Education and Urban Society, 20*, 327–340.

Gay, G. (1990). Achieving educational equity through curriculum design. *Phi Delta Kappan, 70*, 56–62.

Green, T.F. (1984). *The formation of conscience in an age of technology*. Syracuse, NY: School of Education, Syracuse University.

Hilliard III, A.G. (1991–1992). Why we must pluralize the curriculum. *Educational Leadership 49*(4), 12–16.

Hodgkinson, H. (1985). *All one system*. Washington, DC: Institute of Educational Leadership.

Hughes, L. (1975). The negro mother. In L. Haupt L. Heston, & S. Solotaroff (Eds.), *Literature lives* (pp. 74–75). Evanston, IL: McDougal, Littel & Co.

Johnson, D.W., Johnson, R.T., & Holubec, E. (1988). *Cooperation in the classroom*. Edina, MN: Interaction.

Lewis, O. (1975). The children of Sanchez. In L. Haupt L. Heston, & S. Solotaroff (Eds.), *Literature lives* (pp. 271–277). Evanston, IL: McDougal, Littel & Co.

Matthews, M. (1992). Meaningful cooperative learning is the key. *Educational Leadership 50*(6), 64.

Moffitt, J. (1975). To look at anything. In L. Haupt L. Heston, & S. Solotaroff (Eds.), *Literature lives* (p. 471). Evanston, IL: McDougal, Littel & Co.

Noddings, N. (1984). *Caring: A feminine approach to ethics and moral education*. Berkeley: University of California Press.

Oakes, J. (1985). *Keeping track: How schools structure inequality*. New Haven: Yale Univ. Press.

Raywid, M.A. (1989). Community and schools: A prolegomenon. In Giarelli, J. (Ed.). *Philosophy of education* (pp. 2–17). Normal, IL: Philosophy of Education Society.

Sapon-Shevin, M. (1993). Why (even) gifted children need cooperative learning. *Educational Leadership, 50*(6), 62–63.

Slavin, R.E. (1990). *Cooperative learning: Theory, research, and practice*. Englewood Cliffs, NJ: Prentice Hall.

Sleeter, C.E., & Grant, C.A. (1987). An analysis of multicultural education in the United States. *Harvard Educational Review, 57,* 421–444.

Steinbergh, J.W. (1991). To arrive in another world: Poetry, language development, and culture. *Harvard Educational Review, 61,* 51–70.

Williams, D.R. (1990). (Ed.) *Cooperative learning instructional adaptations in reading: A manual of sample lesson plans for the New York State middle school curriculum.* School of Education, Syracuse, New York.

8

Innovative
Classroom
Programs for
Full Inclusion

Jo Jakupcak

Acommitment to celebrating diversity in the classroom is an important philosophical statement for a school district to make. When this commitment is fulfilled, the growth and development of students with special needs is immediately apparent and the social climate of the entire school is positively affected. Initiating such a program, however, presents a formidable challenge in terms of finding pragmatic solutions to the problems posed by a new model.

The inclusion of students with special needs in the general educational setting is an idea whose time has come. Despite the lack of a regular system of networking, schools in many parts of the United States and Canada have all arrived at the same conclusion at the same time: *all* children belong. This chapter describes cooperative learning and demonstrates the power of the cooperative group when peers are used as role models. A description of the implementation of cooperative learning, along with several other practical teaching methods, in the Corvallis Public School District in Montana is used to illustrate the various ways in which the efforts of individual students are encouraged and an atmosphere of group interdependence fostered when such strategies are used.

THE CORVALLIS, MONTANA, PROJECT

History

The Corvallis Public School District is located in a rural area in the Bitterroot Valley of Western Montana, surrounded by towering mountains and heavily forested hills. In 1990 the district had a population of just over 800 students, 86 of whom were receiving resource-room or self-contained special educational services. These programs were carried out from preschool through high school by a special education staff of five teachers, one speech-language professional, a school psychologist/counselor, and a total of six assistants. The special education staff dealt chiefly with students with mobility impairments and students with such a degree of emotional disturbance as to pose a danger to themselves or to others. Several children used wheelchairs and other adaptive equipment. Many required extensive behavioral programs, and one student needed wrap-around services from an array of community resources, including foster placement, social services, and intensive private therapy. Because of the limited size of the staff, services were noncategorical; at each age level, a teacher might expect to work with students with identified emotional, developmental, and/or learning disabilities. Consultants from a larger community nearby shared their expertise in occupational and physical therapy with the local staff members.

In the spring of 1990, word of the trend toward full inclusion of students with disabilities reached Corvallis in the person of Norman Kunc, a Canadian educational consultant and advocate of integration, at a regional meeting of special educators. In a workshop conducted in Kalispell, Montana, he described his experiences as a high school student with cerebral palsy. His underlying message was that all students deserve a "real" education.

While Kunc's initial appeal was emotional, he also cited research evidence to document the failure of pull-out programs. Corvallis educators were already interested in the concept of the integration of students with special needs into the general classroom and curriculum, so, with little formal background knowledge of the methods of integration being tried elsewhere in the country, the staff began to develop schedules, models, and communication tools that would allow the program to be successful. One of the greatest strengths of that first year effort was the support provided by the local school board and by the administration. After the single, day-long workshop given by Norman Kunc, the board, administration, teachers, support personnel, involved parents with an interest in special services, and student body of the junior high and high school were committed to the ideal of helping everyone in the school system to belong. It was in large measure because of this orientation of all concerned parties that the special educators were able to proceed.

Degrees of enthusiasm and willingness to accept new ideas varied, but the message from the administration was clearly that cooperation was expected. New teachers hired over the summer months were immediately introduced to the idea of the inclusion of students with special needs in their classrooms. The agenda for the fall orientation session included time for the special services personnel to approach their general education peers with plans and strategies and to work out the logistics of schedules and shared responsibilities. The special educators scheduled appointments with regular educators during their prep periods, at noontime, and before and after school.

Scheduling was one of the most difficult aspects of the attempt to avoid tracking students with special needs. This meant that special educators had to relinquish daily meetings with some students, and to trust the general educator to carry out a program that they had jointly decided upon. An unexpected difficulty emerged: the special education staff had to share their sense of responsibility with the classroom teachers; the specialist still had the long-term, legal responsibility for meeting individualized education program (IEP) goals, but was no longer in control of the day-to-day activities that would lead to the students' attaining those goals. Many special education teachers experienced feelings of fear and guilt when they turned these duties over to general classroom teachers. They had to ponder both the ethical and legal ramifications of the changes, as well as the emotional impact that they might have on students who had been sheltered in self-contained programs for years.

Conversion of the special educators to the role of consultant was accomplished by year's end, but participants described the change as one of their chief frustrations. The change was achieved only when both general and special educators learned to trust one another and to communicate in efficient ways on a regular basis.

The underlying principle of the Corvallis program is to adapt and adjust the curricula only to the smallest extent necessary for each child. No single method or level of expectation is ever applied to all children with special needs. The goal is to achieve the greatest degree of normalization possible. In the case of a small number of students, the classroom content seems almost irrelevant in terms of their lifelong needs. These students' IEP goals are largely in the fields of communication, vocational training, and adaptive and socialization skills. On the surface, it appears that no amount of adaptation of the general curriculum and no degree of adjustment of the content of the courses would prove useful to these students in their present or future life. Nevertheless, their IEP goals are scrutinized carefully, and ways are sought to implement them within the general classroom. One outstanding example of how general classroom instructors are taking responsibility for students with disabilities is a fourth-grade teacher who declared briskly:

> Sam is missing entirely too much of the discussion time with his friends in his science group. Is there any reason that the physical therapist can't do those stretches on a mat in the reading corner of our room? It would be interesting for the other kids, too.

She then built an entire science unit around the muscles of the human body and integrated the physical therapist and her program into the general curriculum.

Components of Service Delivery

When general and special education teachers began working together in the Corvallis program, the need for three components of a service delivery strategy began to emerge: 1) consultative services, 2) team teaching, and 3) tutorial sessions. Depending on the individual needs of the student, as well as those of classroom teachers, any one approach or combination of approaches might be used.

Consultative Component Under the consultative component, the resource teacher meets regularly with the classroom teacher and provides background information on a student's relevant educational history and skill levels in reading, written language, and mathematics. The specialist, acting as a resource for the classroom teacher, adds information on each student's learning strengths, weaknesses, and preferred learning styles, as well as facts on other subjects that will assist the teacher in determining the best ways to teach that student. Together, they may decide whether to alter curriculum and assessment methods for the student, their expectations for verbal or written output by the student, or the means of encoding or decoding concepts. In the Corvallis program, these adaptations vary greatly according to a student's ability level. In many cases, the special considerations are minimal, such as allowing a student to use a tape recorder to take notes or permitting a student to take tests and quizzes in the resource-room setting.

Even in testing situations, there is a range of possible types of assistance. Some students merely have the test read aloud and then respond to the questions independently. Others are provided with a word bank from which to select the correct responses, while still other students may take only a core portion of each test. Some students who have significant memory problems might use the textbook and their own notes to look up the answers to questions, just as they would for a homework assignment.

General educators are often quite surprised to see that the students do not automatically achieve a high score on such an exercise. Some remark that using the open-book method gives them a much clearer picture of how each student attacks the learning process, and many teachers have used this new insight to alter the methods by which they deliver content material to classes. For example, a secondary school social studies teacher began to use the overhead projector to provide a strategy for notetaking for a student who had difficulties determining the main idea and the primary supporting details of lectures. The teacher presented the strategy in front of the entire class, and the performance of all class members improved because of this child's opportunity to obtain a new study skill.

The special educator works as a team member to adapt and adjust the material being presented and the testing tools being used. When the team of two teachers agrees that such adaptations have seriously altered the scope of what the student has mastered, when he or she deviates greatly from the expected level of mastery for the course, a starred grade (*) is assigned. This symbol for achievement in a significantly altered curriculum was already listed in the Corvallis handbook of policies for dealing with individual differences when the project began. A starred grade indicates a significant change in the level of a student's understanding or in the amount of work that a student produces. For some students, a point system based on documented evidence of their academic functioning levels is assigned. For instance, it might be determined that a student is capable of achieving 70% of the material presented. For this student, grade averages would be figured as they would for all other class members, but then the average would be divided by .70 and a final, starred grade would be recorded. Other students might receive an 80% or a 90% benefit, and so on. There is a danger of patronizing a student who has a known disability, thus lowering expectations for the student and, perhaps, affecting his or her performance. The point system allows some degree of objectivity and helps the teacher avoid the possibility of reverse discrimination, by which teachers might be tempted to assign a grade based on effort and attitude alone.

Many students being served primarily through the consultative component need programs that address their daily behaviors. Negative behavior may stem from motivational problems, emotional needs, or simple organizational deficits. Appropriate programs are designed by special educators after consultation with the general educator, who provides advice on what is needed for success within the classroom setting. These programs are designed to teach and reinforce appropriate social behaviors and correct classroom demeanor. Special services personnel and general educators meet regularly, sometimes informally, to assess the success of the programs and to make changes as the situation demands.

The programs may focus on attention skills, on-task behaviors, homework completion, and appropriate peer interactions. They often take the form of weekly grade checks, daily assignment sheets, and self-monitoring behavior charts that are designed to give students immediate feedback on their interactions in the classroom and with peers.

Team-Teaching Component   Under this component, used particularly in the elementary grades, the specialist and the classroom teacher work together on a regularly scheduled basis. They usually use the general education curriculum, with only minor modifications. The teachers collaborate to teach the entire class, making sure that the needs of atypical students are met through the group activity. Collaboration may take the form of one teacher presenting a lesson while the other is free to attend to the special groups of children who may require repetition of the material, further examples, or practice opportunities, or those who need a more concrete, hands-on approach with additional materials. This method allows for more intensive appraisal of understanding and frees the teachers to attempt more creative projects. In some cases, the two teachers take turns making presentations to the class; in others, they divide the class into smaller groups or use each other to emphasize the importance of what is being taught. For example, one teacher may model questioning techniques for the class, demonstrating to the students that a lecturing teacher may be asked for clarification or elaboration on a point. This is also an excellent opportunity for one teacher to demonstrate notetaking skills while the second teacher presents the concepts in a subject area. The notetaking teacher can ask questions or request a slower pace of delivery, modeling ways in which a student may appropriately approach a classroom teacher for further explanations.

A variation on this team-teaching approach is in use at the secondary level in Corvallis. The schedule of a physical science course includes 1 hour a week for the services of a learning specialist—the resource-room teacher. A variety of topics, ranging from study skills and test-taking strategies to memory-enhancement techniques, are presented at this time to help each student discover his or her own best mode of absorbing new information. The undertaking is being supported by a National Science Teacher's Association grant from the Toyota corporation—the Tapestry Award. The Corvallis project underscores the need to teach all students with its title: "Teach Me To . . . Teach *Me*, Too!" While study skills are being taught within the context of a science class attended by both typical and atypical students, the students identified as having learning problems are showing an amazing ability to succeed alongside their peers with only minimal adaptations of the general curriculum. Because of the project's pre-teaching component, students with learning disabilities have often adopted a leadership role in the science laboratory sessions, guiding typical students through the material. No student has yet received a star designation for his or her grade in the class. The learning goals are met through a combination of pre-teaching, teaching during the general class session, and post-teaching in preparation for tests.

A further refinement, one that is shared by a neighboring school, has students in junior high and high school content area classes spending the final 5 minutes of class each day "journaling." During this time, they jot down three facts learned that day in class, a prediction of what will be taught the following day, and their feelings about the learning process or their achievement levels. Students participating in the program almost immediately began to see themselves as more capable learners, making such observations as, "I wasn't ready for that test. I need to take better notes," or even, "I am failing this course. I'm scared!" (Hanson & Rector, 1991). Such insightful statements, collected weekly, help the team of teachers to zero in on the emotional, study-skill, and subject-skill needs of their students. These mini-journals not only empower the students, but also serve as an effective tool for communication between teachers and students. The teachers using this method estimated that it took less than 10 minutes to scan the study notes of an entire class and assign from 1 to 5 points toward a study-skill bonus in the subject. The point system was designed so that taking good notes all quarter equaled a major test score, which added a strong incentive to complete good journal entries daily.

In team-teaching situations, one or both teachers are able to provide necessary one-to-one time for very specific skills; to group children effectively, such that they can learn from one another; and to create the classroom atmosphere necessary for errorless learning to occur. Members of the team benefit from exposure to the others' ideas in the shared effort to assist all students to learn. Each teacher gives the other confidence to try new ideas. At one point in the year, a seasoned teacher of secondary mathematics remarked, "I've always wanted to make math real and fun for these kids, but I've never had the extra materials and the methods . . . I think I've forgotten how to teach simple addition because I'm usually handling geometry and algebra." This teacher's willingness to try such math tools as calculators, counting rods, and base-10 blocks makes his classroom a fruitful place for high school students who enter general math feeling that they will fail because they're "just no good at arithmetic."

Tutorial Sessions Component   The tutorial sessions component includes individual or small-group study sessions that support the in-class performance of students identified as being at risk. This approach is used in the Corvallis project with students with developmental and learning disabilities. Tutorial strategies vary in the degree of the student's involvement in the general education curriculum. Materials related to various aspects of the lessons—vocabulary words, background information on the topic, and expected precursor concepts—are previewed by the special educator and then taught to the student with special needs. The effect is to enhance the student's comprehension level when the material is later taught to the whole class in the general classroom setting. During a post-teaching session, in preparation for the test on the classroom material, the special educator and the student work together to determine exactly what information in the unit is most important. This technique has been particularly successful in raising the memory and comprehension levels of students who experience weaknesses in both short- and long-term memory.

The student and his or her special education teacher review the student's class notes and the two jointly develop a comprehensive test on the social studies material presented in the middle-school classroom. They then present this test to the classroom teacher, who must approve the content or change it as necessary. The resource teacher prepares this individualized test so that it looks as much like the whole-class test as possible. On exam day, the teacher passes it out when distributing the other tests. Thus, the student is able to take his or her test at the same time and in the same setting as classroom peers. The teacher knows exactly what major concepts have been mastered; the student feels like (and is) a successful class member. Peers view the student as the hard-working, capable learner that he or she is. These procedures provide a sense of sharing and belonging that was formerly missing from these students' educational experience.

Often, curriculum from a student's IEP is embedded within the classroom setting. The special educator may use the tutorial model to pre-teach communication skills, such as appropriate greetings or the proper way to join a discussion. The classroom setting provides the practice opportunity for this skill to be developed; a peer tutor can conduct a practice session.

Educators in the Corvallis project use several different tutorial strategies. For example, a teacher at one of the younger grade levels spends less than 1 hour a day in the resource room. Much of that time is devoted to behavior-management programs, helping individual students to choose daily goals for themselves and learn to monitor their own behaviors, and giving students who come in at the end of the day the motivational rewards that they have earned for making appropriate choices. The rest of the teacher's day is spent in team-teaching and handling small-group practice sessions. Among this teacher's students is one who has a progressive hearing loss. The resource teacher has helped the speech-language therapist to orchestrate signing lessons for entire classes and has arranged for an auditory device that enables the student with hearing loss to use his remaining hearing to communicate with classmates and teachers.

Another teacher, whose caseload is primarily made up of students with disabilities that previously necessitated their being served in a self-contained program, writes individual lesson plans for each student for each class, coordinating the class curricula with the goals listed in the students' IEPs. These highly differentiated plans are carried out with the cooperation of assistants assigned to one or two students. The goal for each student is always the greatest degree of integration possible while still meeting IEP goals. This teacher's role is more that of an educational coordinator who guides a team in carrying out the goals for each child.

Methods

The combination of components (consultative, team teaching, and tutorial) provides a variety of means whereby specialists can support student success within the classroom setting. The various methods or strategies employed in the classroom also play an important role in the probability of a student's success in the individualized program. Some strategies that are particularly effective are cross-curricular teaching; cooperative learning; peer-tutor programs, including the establishment of friendship circles; and the use of available technology. The Corvallis program uses each of these tools to some degree, with modifications dictated by a student's individual needs.

Cross-Curricular Teaching   The general education staff of the Corvallis school system serves students with special needs according to the pervasive philosophy of mutual support. Staff members may already be familiar with team-teaching and cross-curricular approaches at many levels: the library staff, for example, provide collections of materials (texts, posters, videos, and other audio-visual media) to expand and enhance teachers' presentations on specific subjects. Teachers of different grade-levels join forces to produce medieval fairs, newspapers in the classroom, and mini-course days. This year, three secondary school departments coordinated their assignments: the earth science course assigned a term paper on the geology of the local area, the geography course focused on the landforms of the state, and the English course was devoted to the writing of research papers. This cohesive unit allowed students to experience the knowledge, comprehension, and application levels of learning. They learned from three relevant skill areas in such an integrated way that the time required was only one-third of that which would have been required had each department presented the material separately. The students with memory problems had the benefit of hearing many of the same concepts three times and were able to put these facts to immediate use. The success level was also enhanced, as evidenced by the students' scores in all three subject areas.

Cooperative Learning   Cooperative group learning is a teacher-initiated strategy used within the general classroom that encourages the acquisition of social skills and communication capabilities and enhances employment preparation. It provides opportunities for practicing appropriate decisionmaking skills relevant to the use of leisure and recreation time. The power of a cooperative group, using the peer role models, is perhaps one of the most efficient behavior-shaping techniques in education today. Behavior shaping takes place almost effortlessly when a student has the strong motivation of wanting to be accepted by his or her classmates. In a guided session that supports group interdependence, each student is encouraged by teacher and peers to participate fully in each project. Students are taught specific techniques for praising others' ideas and are coached in positive feedback and group unity. Each child is assessed in terms of the quality of his or her interactions within the group, as well as performance on the subject matter being taught. Through the consideration of individual opinions and consensus-reaching, this practice fosters a spirit of mutual support and promotes an atmosphere of tolerance for differences. In this accepting atmosphere, every student has the opportunity to express feelings and to posit answers without fear of rejection, as it is a less stressful situation than those that traditional competitive learning formats create.

The Corvallis school administration advocated the exploration of cooperative teaching techniques. In order to upgrade teaching skills in this area, the administration provided support in the form of cost-free workshops for teachers at all grade levels. Cooperative learning methods, derived from the work of Johnson and Johnson (1986), were taught in two day-long workshops and were offered in more depth through an extension course from the nearby University of Montana. The extension courses were held at the rural school setting, aiding many teachers for whom transportation to the university might otherwise have proven a problem. Advancement on the salary scale for completing the coursework was approved, and teachers from all grade levels took advantage of the educational opportunity. The classroom results proved the coursework to be beneficial. Students who had previously turned in few or no assignments began to participate, and positive peer pressure helped disorganized students remember to bring their parts of projects to class so that they would not let the group down.

When one science teacher was praised for his flexibility in adopting a new method of teaching for use with what has traditionally been viewed as a content-driven subject area, he responded, "I've been teaching my labs as cooperative groups of two and three for years. We just never called it 'cooperative learning' before now!" Another teacher accepted the change more readily after he reflected how often he, in his adult professional life, was called upon to work on committees to bring about change. Many teachers who initially expressed doubts about cooperative learning groups came to view them as a new strength in their teaching repertoire. Following Johnson and Johnson's (1986) advice, approximately 25%–30% of teaching time is given to the use of this technique. Lecture time, individual practice time, and some individual assessment are still seen as valuable.

In the cooperative learning groups, the teacher places a heterogeneously balanced mixture of students together and assigns a rotating role to each. Thus, each student in a group of three or four gets the opportunity to practice the skills of leading, recording, and encouraging others. The experience of relating to others in a positive manner occurs within an established group, with the support and security that comes from having worked together previously. The growth of trust, interdependence, a sense of responsibility to others, and self-esteem is almost visible. Few students remain isolated and uninvolved in such a setting. This provides the kind of social-skills practice needed by all students, and particularly by the student with special needs.

Peer Tutoring   A third method used in Corvallis schools is the peer tutor and cross-age peer tutor program. The special service providers in the program approach the general education students through a series of disability-awareness sessions. At each grade level, age-appropriate activities are provided for the classrooms. These included the "Kids on the Block" puppet show, disability adoption day, films, and talks. A special effort was made to avoid a patronizing attitude.

One of the most successful concepts adopted was Robert Perske's *Friendship Circle* (1988). In this model, the entire class uses brainstorming techniques to try to understand the dreams and fears of a class member who has special needs. When it is possible to do so with dignity and sensitivity, the student with special needs and/or a parent may become a part of this procedure. The circle often addresses the curiosity and fears of students who may be unfamiliar with persons with disabilities. It provides a forum for questions and a model for discussion about differences. It suggests positive roles for interactions and builds a support system for the students to use. At the end of the session, volunteers are assigned to a particular circle of friends for a student with special needs and either the special educator or the classroom teacher, or both, plan specific activities in which the circle of friends may help the student with special needs. The latter may be playtime activities or study-buddy exercises. A study-buddy may make a carbon set of notes for a student with a physical limitation, for example, or may arrange to type or tape a report. The friend may provide physical assistance for getting to and from the lunchroom or playground. In some classrooms, these services become sought-after jobs assigned to student volunteers on a rotating basis.

In Corvallis, some form of peer-tutoring system was employed at all age levels. Generally, it was used with age-peers in order to enhance their sense of belonging in a class. In a few instances, peer tutoring was performed by an older student who acted as a teacher's assistant for a younger pupil. An effective pairing was made between a high school student with a learning disability and a much younger student with a severe cognitive delay and physical disability. One outcome of this relationship was a career choice; the older student decided to become a physical therapist's assistant. Two high school students who had resisted several behavioral programs designed to motivate them to complete academic assignments finally became productive students in order to earn the privilege of spending an hour per day helping a younger student. A parent called during finals week to remark, "I don't know what you've done to him! He insisted on coming to school even though he has the flu. He said something about having to pass his exams so he could keep his tutoring job." Three months earlier this student spent most of each class period slouched in the back of classrooms with his coat collar turned up to hide his face and his nose in a fantasy book.

With rare exceptions, the degree of acceptance of the integrated students has been overwhelming. Students report the triumphs of their peers to the special educators; the atmosphere is one of pride in others' accomplishments. A favorite phrase often heard is a conspiratorial, "J__'s smarter than you know!"

Assistive Technology   Another classroom method used to make inclusion work is the effective use of available technology. Possible equipment ranges from such low-tech devices as adaptive spoons and trays to make self-feeding possible to a computer lab that allows students to work on individualized adaptations to spelling lists or math skills while the class works on the same skill at a different level. At the junior and senior high school levels, software is available for students with limited reading ability or rudimentary math skills to do supported drafting designs. A word-processing program makes it possible for students with learning disabilities to express themselves effectively without being penalized for spelling errors that occur because of perceptual problems. A computer with a built-in CD-ROM encyclopedia teaches basic library-research skills with a minimum of teachers' time and effort. These tools work together to make each student the most independent learner possible. Students who read at a markedly different rate than their peers qualify to apply to Talking Books for the Blind. Textbooks and recreational reading will be recorded and a specially equipped tape recorder will be provided without cost once initial membership as a person with a reading disability is attained. Textbooks that are played on a computer with voice-out capabilities are also available for these students.

OTHER PLACES, OTHER PROGRAMS

Homecoming Project

The inclusion concept has also been piloted and adopted as policy in the state of Vermont, where it is embodied in the "Homecoming" project, referring to the reversal of the practice of sending students with disabling conditions to specialized residential learning centers (Fox et al., 1986). The State Education Department, in cooperation with their Center for Developmental Disabilities and local school districts, has placed students with severe disabilities in their home school districts, emphasizing the benefits to students in both affective and academic areas. Vermont makes use of core-planning teams; access to consultants and inservice training for regular educators are provided by the state. Core-planning teams are made up of staff members in local school districts. This team has responsibility for assessing individual student needs, writing IEPs, and easing the transition of each student into a general classroom program. The team has the further responsibility of placing each student at a post-graduate level.

In addition to the core-planning team, each district has an on-sight consultant and access to the State of Vermont Interdisciplinary Team for Intensive Special Education. These resources are available for inservice assistance, consultation as difficulties arise, and technical assistance for the planning team and general education staff. The pilot year for this project was 1983, when a 3-year federally funded grant was received. As of 1986, 56 students in Vermont had been relocated from regional learning centers to their home school districts. This move involved students of all age levels in 26 school districts. Policymakers in Vermont feel that the program is so successful that they have adopted home-district placement for all learners as a primary goal of special education (Fox et al., 1986).

Syracuse Project

A variety of attempts at inclusion have been made in the state of New York. One of the most interesting is that of the Edward Smith School in Syracuse. Here, in 1986–1987, a group of 4th-grade teachers volunteered to enroll one or two students with autism in their general education classrooms. While a number of approaches were used, the single most successful one was a teaming approach in which at least one of the teachers was dually certified in general and special education. The team of two teachers then divided their daily schedule so that each taught for part of the day in each classroom. Both classes contained one or more students with autism. While in a classroom, the teacher was completely responsible for all of the children. The chief advantage, as determined by the instructors, was that neither teacher identified more closely with the typical or atypical children. The social effect on peers was positive in that all pupils perceived the teachers as treating each student equally. This model is being considered for use at other grade levels (Fenwick, 1987).

C-O BOCES Project

Prior to 1985, in Auburn, New York, students with severe disabilities were served in specialized centers (Giangreco, 1986). As of 1992, the rural educational cooperatives of Cayuga-Onondaga Board of Cooperative Educational Services (C-O BOCES) has served 110 students with severe disabilities in age-appropriate settings in public schools. They plan to increase the percentage of students served within their home districts from 70% to 100% within the next few years. Home-school service is accomplished through a combination of placing students with extensive needs in classes with students with less-severe disabilities (but still identified as having some special needs) and/or part time in heterogeneous classes with support. The policy of dispersal is such that the classroom population is proportionate to the general school population.

An unusual feature of the Auburn program is the placement of 18- to 21-year-old students at Cayuga Community College. Here students with disabilities use college facilities, interact with age-appropriate peers, and share work—study sites. They receive instruction on campus and participate in job-related and leisure-time experiences in the larger community (Giangreco, McKinney, Fitzpatrick, & Sabin, 1986).

Ontario Project

The philosophy of Education for Community Living (ECL) has been adopted in many parts of Ontario, Canada (Forest, 1984). The goal is to merge special and general education and to offer a program to all students, be they gifted, average in ability, or in need of remediation. School boards from several districts, and especially the Hamilton—Wentworth Separate School Board and the Wellington County Separate School Board, have included students who exhibit extreme and disruptive behaviors in general classes. They use a team approach, and obtain community resources and consult specialists as necessary. The local school district's principal is the administrator, and the rest of the team is made up of general and special educators, with additional personnel called upon as needed. Responsibility for teaching all children is shared. An area of primary emphasis is the need of all students to experience social growth and normalized human interactions. Support circles are formed, and care is taken that these circles are large enough that no one person is unduly burdened with the care of another. This is seen as a mutually beneficial community activity that enhances the life of each individual involved (Snow & Forest, 1985).

Stratham School Project

"The Classroom is the Resource" is the title of an article describing the success of educators and students at the Stratham Memorial School in Stratham, New Hampshire when the staff experimented with integrating students with disabilities into the general education classroom (Wansart, 1990). This change came about with a minimum of pre-planning and within a 2-week period in January 1989, as the result of classrooms that were process oriented and student centered. The fourth- and fifth-grade teachers had been using a studio approach to teach writing. The success of this program led the teachers to look at their reading program, which resulted in the district revamping its approach to reading. It adopted an individualized program that contained elements of choice, sharing results in small groups as well as whole-class settings, and heterogeneous groupings and peer collaboration in both reading and the writing process. Special educators, noting that this success was individually based, asked to include some students who had been identified as having learning disabilities. The students' progress convinced the staff to attempt integration schoolwide. The program included three components: student support, direct instruction, and teacher support. Student support involved adding a special educator to the collaborative reading–writing process. This person attended work sessions two to four times weekly, noting specific skill needs, whether in the area of phonics, spelling, or comprehension. Then direct instruction targeting specific skills and using the student's own choice of reading material or a recent writing sample was scheduled in 15-minute daily sessions. A classroom aide or either teacher (general or special) gave this individual lesson. The third component, teacher support, was provided by a scheduled classroom aide who was assigned to any duty except the direct teaching of an identified student with a disability. Thus, the classroom teacher was freed to spend this extra time with individual students. All teachers participating in the project came to be more directly involved in the attainment of literacy by all students, and students' skills in the language arts grew beyond expected levels. The current plan is to expand the program to other subject areas (Wansart, 1990).

CONCLUDING COMMENTS

The Corvallis staff believe that the components (consultative, team-teaching, and tutorial) for ensuring successful inclusion are working well. The classroom methods—cross-curricular teaching, cooperative group learning, peer tutoring, and assistive technology—are now in common usage. The next goal is to refine each approach and technique and evaluate the efficiency of each. A major part of that endeavor will be to examine the programs being used elsewhere. Anecdotes from schools that have worked to include students with special needs are positive. We plan to conduct further systematic research to identify factors that support the inclusion of students with special needs in the general classroom.

It is to be hoped that definitive studies in specific skill areas will be conducted in order to provide the necessary documentation to support this exciting trend in the education of all students. It is important to note that no single component was a factor in all of the successes cited. Perhaps the very diversity of approaches, the fact that each is a local device, with the attendent pride of ownership, is a strength in itself. While most who participate in these programs share an enthusiasm for what they are doing, they also share a belief in the ongoing, evolutionary nature of the process. Just as we celebrate the diversity of the learners involved, perhaps we should also celebrate the diversity of the individuals working on the programs, and even the diversity of the programs themselves.

REFERENCES

Fenwick, V. (1987). The Edward Smith School Program: An integrated public school continuum for autistic children. In M.S. Berres & P. Knoblock (Eds.), *Program models for mainstreaming: Integrating students with moderate to severe disabilities*. Rockville, MD: Aspen Publishers, Inc.

Forest, M., (1984). Education update: The Wellington Country Separate School Board at work. In M. Forest (Ed.), *Education integration: A collection of readings on the integration of children with mental handicaps into regular school systems* (pp. 71–75). Downsview, Ontario, Canada: National Institute on Mental Retardation.

Fox, W., Thousand, J., Williams, W., Fox, T., Towne, P., Reid, R., Conn-Powers, C., & Calcagni, L. (1986). *Educating learners with severe handicaps*. Burlington: Center for Developmental Disabilities, University of Vermont.

Giangreco, M.F. (1986). *Northeast BOCES Integration Project survey results*. Unpublished document. Ithaca, NY: Tompkins-Seneca-Tioga Board of Cooperative Educational Services.

Giangreco, M.F., McKinney, P., Fitzpatrick, M., & Sabin, C.A. (1986). *Initiating change at the local level: Delivery of services to students with moderate to profound handicapping conditions*. Auburn, NY: Cayuga-Onondaga Board of Cooperative Educational Services (ERIC Document Reproduction Service No., ED 276 182)

Hanson, K., & Rector, M.N. (1991). *Meeting the needs of all children within the regular classroom*. Workshop, Missoula County High School, Missoula, Montana.

Johnson, D., & Johnson, R.T. (1986). Mainstreaming and Cooperative Learning Strategies. *Exceptional Children, 52,* 553–561.

Perske, R. (1988). *Circles of friends*. Nashville: Abingdon Press.

Snow, J., & Forest, M. (1985). *Support circles: Building a vision*. Unpublished man-
    uscript. Downsview, Ontario, Canada, G. Allen Roehrer Institute.
Wansart, W.L. (1990). The classroom is the resource. *Intervention in School and
    Clinic, 26*(1), 48–51.

Index